In the Twinkling of His Eye

Man's Last Days on Earth

Peachey

WESTBOW
PRESS®
A DIVISION OF THOMAS NELSON
& ZONDERVAN

All Scripture quotations are from the Authorized King James Version (KJV).

WestBow Press books may be ordered through booksellers or by contacting:

WestBow Press
A Division of Thomas Nelson & Zondervan
1663 Liberty Drive
Bloomington, IN 47403
www.westbowpress.com
1 (866) 928-1240

ISBN: 978-1-4908-3504-4 (sc)
ISBN: 978-1-4908-3505-1 (e)

Library of Congress Control Number: 2014907351

Print information available on the last page.

WestBow Press rev. date: 01/31/2020

In an instantaneous moment, without warning God's glory, his grace, love, mercy, and power will be manifested to his people and an unbelieving world. Time will cease to exist for many, and there will be no future to look forward to on planet earth.

ACKNOWLEDGEMENT

I want to give a special acknowledgement to my mom and sister, Wendy, for their faith and encouragement as I wrote this book. It was not easy for them to accept my move to Missouri so that this book could be written.

I dedicate this book to my heavenly Father for without his love, mercy and Gift of Knowledge this book never could have been written. I thank him for his grace filled plan that established his presence in my life, for without him my life would be empty and meaningless.

I pray that everyone who reads this book will be filled with the peace that passes all understanding in Jesus name.

PREFACE

"My life exists in all the universe, without me there is nothing. Have you accepted my only son, Jesus? He is everything; or are you nothing? Satan will challenge his right to everything on earth, including man. My son purchased those that accepted his sacrifice on the cross. It is the only way to fight this challenge that is coming. Can man alone fight Satan? Was not he my cherubim? This last battle for man will be epic. Thus sayeth the Lord."

Many revelations have been given to me throughout the years, and in this book I will be passing onto you some of the prophecies and words of knowledge given to me, such as the destruction of two major cities in the United States. One of the cities to be destroyed is located in Texas and the other is located in Louisiana, yet the Lord has a plan to save these two states. Perilous times are coming.

The bible says, in I Thessalonians 5:3 (KJV), "For when they shall say, peace and safety; then sudden destruction cometh upon them, "as travail upon a woman with child; and they shall not escape."

As people are going about their daily lives, a suddenly

event will take place that will engulf and cause great sorrow for the human race. An event never dreamed of will strike. The Holy Spirit gave me a vision of a coming event that will transform all of mankind.

To prepare me for this future event, I experienced an encounter with God at the age of 16. This was not something a person would seek out, or plan to happen; but the Lord God Almighty came into my room one night, and fear and respect for him would enter into my being.

CONTENTS

CHAPTER 1

Introduction

This book has been a challenging book to write. The Lord has spoken to me many times about things to include in this book. In the first part of my book the Lord witnessed to me he wanted to write Chapter 12, called The Final Word because he desired to talk to his people and I wrote the words down, word for word as he gave them to me.

Jesus' final words on the cross were, "It is finished." He knew and understood that man's final days were going to be perilous and trying. He had done all he could do to reach multitudes of people with his message of hope and salvation that would be passed down throughout history. Will man trust God in their final hours on earth, as the anti-Christ grows stronger and man enters into the tribulation times? Will he grow closer to the Lord, or will he be one of those who are offended and falls away just before Christ's return?

Events such as those described in the book of Revelation are soon to be unleashed in order for us to know our Lord and Savior. An epic battle between man and Satan will take place. Multitudes of angels will be released to help his believers fight the battle ahead. Even now these powerful angels stand at attention with their flaming swords raised high, eager to intervene on behalf of those that have accepted Jesus as Savior.

Many people will focus on the horrific events described in the book of Revelation instead of focusing on its true purpose, the unveiling of Jesus Christ. Earthly blessings and the sin in people's life have stopped the relationship with Jesus from coming into being with many of his people, especially those in the United States. One of the changes to take place will be the setting of Christians free from the past, present, and future; bringing them into a place where they live in the presence of their Lord. Jesus desires a relationship with his children, he does not want lip service.

A lot of people are a product of their environment and the Lord plans to bring healing to them. Many lives will be changed and Jesus will establish an army of believers to help his people. Joseph was moved out of his safe environment to provide food for his family, Moses was moved out of his surroundings to free his people from slavery and bondage, Esther 's life was changed in order for her to help save her people from death and destruction. Daniel was moved out of his homeland and everything that was familiar to him and he went into captivity to give testimony of God's greatness, power and authority over all the earth.

When God came down to talk with Moses on the mountain, the environment changed; there were clouds. Look at all the plagues the Egyptians went through, it changed their environment. The Israelites walked on dry land through the red sea. The waters divided and the environment was changed. Jesus rebuked the waves when there was a storm.

The storm was an event that caused fear but Jesus brought peace and calm into that situation. Jesus showed the apostles they could walk in the miraculous, by his example of walking on water. Man's environment will soon change drastically all around him as a "Suddenly" event happens. This "Suddenly" event will cause many people to ask, "How can anything good happen out of anything so bad?"

Fear and sorrow unlike anything anyone has ever known will strike into the hearts of everyone. An unknown event is going to take place that will change all nations on the face of the earth. Yet in the midst of all this, God will manifest his glory to those who are his, and those who seek him. Jesus will wrap his loving arms around his people bringing peace and comfort to them amidst the chaos, death and destruction that is coming. He will provide his people with the keys of his spiritual kingdom to help them through their trying hour, to help them endure. Many of the experiences I have gone through led me to an understanding of this coming event, and a knowing of how it will affect mankind.

I had a fairly normal childhood. My family did not have a lot of money and my dad worked three jobs to support us. There were five of us siblings and we all grew up independent. I was the introvert in the family. You could usually find me somewhere, sitting quietly in a corner, reading a book. On the average I read one or two books a day.

The decisions I made early on in my life brought me sorrow and great destruction. I married at the age of 22. I remember seeing in the spiritual realm a very dark ominous cloud fill the church during my marriage ceremony. At that time, I did not realize what I was seeing, or what it represented.

I thought I had married the man of my dreams and that I had married into a wonderful supporting family; but I was soon to learn it was an illusion. Instead I learned I had married an angry man who was mentally abusive, a man who demanded total control over my life. I found his family to be a close knit family whose acceptance and support was conditional based on their own family standards. My counselor called this type of family a mesh family. If you married one, you married them all.

My family was accepting of all others no matter what they looked like, or what they believed; but my ex-husband's family judged everyone by their standards of looks, education, and ambition in life, etc. If you did not think or act like they did you were put down and belittled behind your back. My ex-husband use to call his mother "Piggy" to her face and "oink" at her because he thought she was a little heavy. My former sister-in-law's ex-husband was called stupid behind his back because he was not ambitious enough. His career as a teacher did not fit into the family mold.

Soon after we were married we started our family and over a period of five years we had four beautiful daughters.

My ex-husband had a way with words that stabbed the heart. He knew just what to say that would hurt you the most. His words and the mental abuse I suffered ended up causing me partial amnesia. One morning I could not take any more of his cruel words and his adultery, and my mind just snapped. There was no warning that absolute terror was going to happen to me. It was like someone snapped their fingers and in an instant my world ended. A lot of the memories of my childhood and marriage were gone, and ties to many friends and loved ones were severed. I had isolated memories of events but I seemed disassociated from them. When I tried to remember my past it felt like a vise being squeezed around my head. The harder I tried to remember the tighter the vise became until I stopped trying to remember. The only true peace I had was thinking about Jesus. I associated the feeling of a vise being squeezed about my head with the crown of thorns that was placed upon the head of Jesus and the pain he felt as it sat upon his head.

I actually thank the Lord for removing a lot of my recollections because who wants tormenting memories to be a part of their life. For over 30 years whenever the thought of my ex-husband would came to my mind, there was a feeling of abject terror that would rise up within me. There was no memory of any particular event that would trigger this feeling, just the thought of my being anywhere near him; yet most of the time the Lord kept me from fear. After 30 years that emotional response of terror has finally ended.

My emotional state not only caused trouble with past memories but current memories as well. I could look at my watch to see the time, but a second later I could not remember what time it was. Many memories from that point on would quickly fade away as each day passed. As the years went by my memory would improve, but it was never as sharp and clear as it once was. I had been permanently changed.

But the most remarkable thing that happened to me was I no longer felt the "literal" sense of time itself, not beyond the day I was living in. For me, time literally ceased to exist. I learned to accept each day as it came and not to look beyond it. I believe one of the blessings the Lord gave to me as a result of what happened was his revelations about the concept of time.

A lot of time people want to know why a person of abuse does not leave. My answer would be because you do not think rationally. You don't realize the damage being done to you. You know you are going through hurt and you feel tremendous hurt, but beyond that you don't recognize that your mental processes are damaged. Not until I was totally removed from the situation did healing begin. Once my healing began then I could start making rational decisions.

Jesus never left me, not even once. He has manifested his presence to me and I have been blessed to know the reality of his presence and the revelations of God as I walked in his glory. I can only describe my life as walking in a different reality, the spiritual reality. If there was a hole between heaven and earth, I had one foot in each and felt each. It was very difficult to learn to live in both realities at the same time. I kept many things to myself. I felt people could not understand what had happened to me, nor would they know how to deal with it, or how to react to it. I found myself emotionally and spiritually handicapped. I think I was spiritually handicapped in that I was thrust into my spiritual world as an adult and missed the slow growth that comes out of childhood.

Because the Lord's glory and grace was poured out upon me, I dwelt under the shadow of the Almighty. I learned that Jesus will pour out as much grace and glory as you need to go through any situation, even if it means walking in the miraculous 24 hours a day. Jesus became everything to me and I held on to him with all of my being.

Because I lost ties to my family members, I became tied to

Jesus. I was like a newborn baby being raised by my heavenly Father here on earth, growing and becoming familiar with his presence first.

As the Father God revealed different aspects of himself to me, I would be healed in those very same areas of my mind, will, and emotions. An example would be an agreement. Jesus spoke to me and said that he and the Father were in agreement over me. This happened in order to remove that spirit of separation and divorce that had become a part of my life, to create unity and wholeness within me. As I experienced different reflection of the Father God, I came to know him and I came to know myself. Walking in the miraculous became very natural to me, as natural as breathing.

I learned things about life that very few people will understand; such as where does the will to live comes from, the trauma a baby's undergoes as it is born, and trauma of abortion and what judgment the world will face for allowing it. I was shown the most difficult process to go through in life is going from teenager to adult, because that is when teenagers are discovering who they are and choosing who they will grow into as an adult; and the key to this transition is knowing Jesus. To know Jesus is to know yourself. As Jesus filled my life with his presence I learned I could trust him, that he is gentle, loving, and kind.

Was it easy to live through this, NO; but the Lord sent me two friends to help me through this time. They never saw me as broken or damaged, but as extremely hurt. You will find in this book how to walk in the miraculous each and every second of your life. You will discover wonderful words of knowledge that will bring blessings and healings to your inner most being. You will know that a miracle exists inside of you and surrounds you, and how the Lord's abundant knowledge will help you to face the future.

A time of miracles is coming to the earth, miracles that will bring glory to our Lord. This book will talk of end time events, but the Lord would have me give them to you from the perspective of the emotional and spiritual impact, not the physical realm.

It was difficult to write this book because there are so many pieces missing in me, things I still can't remember. I know my ex-husband refused to let me see my dad as he was dying from cancer but most of those memories are not within me. I do remember his one and only apology ever given to me during our years of marriage was of his refusing to let me be with my dad before his death. This occurred after his own father died.

You will understand as you read this book that what happened to me was actually foretold to me at the age of 16 when the Father God entered my bedroom one night.

I was thinking about a particular end time book when the Holy Spirit witnessed to me there would be a flood of end time hate books being published. I was a little surprise that he would call end-time books hate books. I asked him why did he call them hate books, and he said it is because man hates to see these things coming.

The Father God wants his people to focus on and see events as he sees them and not just as man sees them. He wants his people to know they can trust him. He not only desires that his people know the signs and the times that will take place, but he wants them to understand and know why these things are happening. Jesus wants to filter out the fear, lies and hatred that will descend upon his children. The Father God desires that mankind focus on Jesus, his only son, and not merely on the devastating judgments that will be unleashed as he allows these things to happen.

People sense deep within their spiritual being that something unheard of is gathering and approaching, but they don't quite know what it is. Jesus knowing the future is preparing to battle on behalf of those that are his, and those that will soon belong to him. He is asking mankind to choose who they will serve; and he is pleading with his people to give up the sin in their life.

John in the seven letters to the seven churches in the book of Revelation warned all the churches to get right with the Lord. Jesus knew what they were going through, what was in their hearts, their strengths and weaknesses, and that man had a choice to make that would determine his future and eternal destination. Would man hear and listen to what the Lord is saying about the sin in his life, or would man reject the Lord's counsel?

The Father God loves his children so very much, and it grieves him to see them hurting themselves and hurting others. He wants to set the captives free, but sometimes they don't want to be free. Jesus is coming back for a spotless bride, not one that compromises and gives in to sin. There is a cleansing coming to the Lord's people.

Jesus himself will reach down and begin removing the filth and dirt that stubbornly clings to his people as war rages all around. This cleansing will cause great changes to take place in the hearts and minds of his people.

As a new resolve comes to the Lord's people to serve him at any cost, a mighty army is going to raise up that will do mighty exploits. This boldness of end time believers will stun the world into amazement as signs and wonders begin manifesting the glory of the Lord.

As events take place, some people will lose just about everything they have, yet they will praise and worship their God for he will supernaturally sustain them. As the Lord removes those things that separate his people from himself, mankind will learn that the Lord's presence and closeness to them is their greatest reward. They will find that belonging to him and walking beside him is worth the loss of everything here on earth.

Jesus will no longer be an UNKNOWN GOD. He will be the center of their existence and being, and he will add blessings to their life that will glorify him. Does Jesus dwell in only a few small areas of your life instead of dwelling within all of your being? In his presence there is peace and joy. Are you being robbed of peace and joy in areas that you have excluded him from?

How many of the Lord's people will be a part of the great falling away, because in their minds they believed they would escape all judgment that is soon coming upon the earth? Even when they see the examples of the Christians in the Middle East and elsewhere being killed, the starvation in Africa, and devastating earthquakes in Haiti and Japan; the people in the United States have a hard time believing that anything on a nationwide scale will ever happen to them here.

My family began going through tribulation experiences many years ago. A lady came up to my mom and dad in church and prophesied to them that our family would go through difficult times, but we would all be blessed and saved. Just before my dad died he passed on a vision to our family. He was shown that everyone in our family that was alive at the time of his death was going to be with the Lord when their life on earth ended.

Not long ago, I was given a vision of panicked sheep running around a huge rock in absolute terror. Amongst the sheep are riding three horsemen. Two of the riders and their horses were fully visible, but the third rider and his horse were only partially visible. The sheep represents those that belong to the Lord. The riders, riding upon their horses amidst this stampede, are the first horsemen of the apocalypse.

The first horse mentioned in the book of Revelations is the white horse, and the rider is wearing a victor's crown. He will conquer many people through peace and he is a gifted speaker. This is the spirit of the anti-Christ and he will bring death and destruction of incomprehensible levels upon mankind. The second horse mentioned is fiery red. The horseman upon this horse brings war, death, and destruction on a world wide scale. The third horse is black and its rider brings great famine upon the face of the earth. We are close to seeing this third rider very soon. Mankind has reached the tipping point for judgment and soon will slide into the abyss.

What is this "Suddenly event" that is soon going to strike at the hearts of everyone on earth causing fear and panic?

CHAPTER 2

A Suddenly

The bible says, in I Thessalonians 5:3 (KJV), "For when they shall say, peace and safety; then sudden destruction cometh upon them, "as travail upon a woman with child; and they shall not escape."

As people are going about their daily lives, a suddenly event will take place that will engulf and cause great sorrow for the human race. An event never dreamed of will strike. The Holy Spirit gave me a vision of a coming event that will transform all of mankind.

In this vision I was standing on a hill top next to an angel. My hand was gently placed on the angel's left arm. The scripture comes to me, "Who hath believed our report? And to whom is the arm of the Lord revealed?" (Isaiah 53:1 KJV) I was standing quietly next to this messenger of the Lord with peace filling my entire being. My eyes were drawn to look out over the city before me. This city could have been Seattle, New York, Dallas, or any city. It was an emblematic city, with the sun warmly shining down on it. I saw the busy city center with sky scrapers built like tall monoliths packed tightly together. There were various small to medium sized businesses located on many streets throughout the city, and there were crowded neighborhoods of homes located on the outskirts of the city, and a few homes scattered within. I could see sparsely growing trees and vegetation. Men, women and children were going about their lives like it was just another ordinary day.

As I looked in the distance I saw an enormous wall of water, greater than any tsunami you could possible imagine and higher than any building headed straight towards this city. There was no warning. All of a sudden it was there and it was going to cover the land everywhere in an instant. There was no place to run and there was no escape from it, as there was no time. There was no shelter strong enough to keep the wall of water out. No building tall enough to rise above it. No one was going to escape, not rich or poor, young man or old man, women or child. All I had time for as I was standing there was to quickly pray, "Lord, forgive me of all my sins," because I knew I wasn't going to make it as well.

Jesus will give answers to his people as they cry out to him when this event happens. He will pour out his glory upon his children not only to save them, but to teach them his word and set them free. It will not be easy for the Lord's people to face the impact this event will have in their life. The scriptures say that all have sinned and come short of the glory of the Lord. Jesus loves his people so very much and he wants to help them overcome the sin in their life. These over-comers will learn to praise him through much sorrow, as tears are running down their faces and their hearts are breaking.

His knowledge and truth will pour out upon his followers.

Self-righteousness will be removed. A deeper level of forgiveness will become such a deep-rooted part of his people that they will be able to release those that have deeply wounded and hurt them, into the love and blessings of the Lord. His word says, forgive, and ye shall be forgiven." (Luke 6:37 KJV) Each person will be reminded of the cross and the price that Jesus paid for them there.

Remember when Jesus passed by the man who was lame? Jesus healed him but warned him not to sin again or a worse thing would come upon him. (John 5:14) Jesus saw that the issue of forgiveness and turning away from sin needed to be dealt with if man was to escape a second and worse judgment.

This event whether its total worldwide financial collapse, the Middle East erupting into war, or the mark of the beast, whatever this wall of water represents we will all have to face it and no one will escape.

Jesus felt great sorrow just before he went to the cross, because he knew what was coming. He was in so much agony that he wept drops of blood. Mathew 26:38 (KJV) says, "My soul is exceeding sorrowful, even unto death." The Lord sees the sin and filth that covers his children, and the pride and rebellion that is inside the hearts of those that belong to him. Jesus wasn't just feeling sorrow for what he knew he would endure on the cross, but for what he knew people would endure and face because of sin. His death on the cross and what he suffered would impart to his people great strength when they were weak, and a steadfastness of spirit that would carry them through their time of sorrow as they faced their cross.

The will of many will change. Christians will no longer

live for themselves but for God and to partake of the life he offers them. The sorrow God's children will go through will lead to repentance and life, but to the ungodly it will bring them to spiritual death. There is a living truth that says, "God is not the God of the dead, but of the living" (Matthew 22:32 KJV). Those that choose and accept life will embrace the giver of life Jesus, but those that choose and accept death will embrace the giver of death the anti-Christ. There will be no middle ground, no living in both worlds. The bible says in II Samuel 22:38 (KJV), "And the afflicted people thou wilt save." The Lord will give great grace to his children as they follow him.

CHAPTER 3

A Revealing

Jesus is in love with his creation. He created man to have a unique and intimate relationship with him, but man has been hiding from him ever since they walked together in the Garden of Eden. The first to hide were Adam and Eve after listening to the lies Satan told them about eating of the forbidden fruit. (Genesis 3) Since the very beginning of man's existence on earth man has had to decide who to believe, their creator or Satan.

The spirit of the anti-Christ has been growing over the years. As the Lord's people are bombarded with ungodly lies, Christians once again will have to choose who they will believe, Jesus or Satan. Those that choose to believe Satan will turn away from their Lord and try to convince others to believe in his lies. Even so, Jesus will plead with his people to turn back to him before it is too late.

As people get deeper into sin, many will be turned over to a reprobate mind, but there is still hope for them.

One of the reasons my marriage failed was that my ex-husband and I were unequally yoked. Our marriage lasted about 15 years. Part of my divorce settlement was that I was given a truck that was only a few months old. At that time I did not know there was such a thing as gap insurance, and my truck was stolen. I was broken hearted because I did not know how I was to financially come out of this situation.

About a week after it had been stolen, I was praying and the Holy Spirit spoke to me and said, "Bind the reprobate mind." This upset me at first as I thought maybe I had been turned over to a reprobate mind in some area of my life. Then I realized the Holy Spirit wanted me to pray and bind the reprobate mind of the person that had stolen my truck. I obeyed the Lord, and within 12 hours the person that had stolen my truck had returned it and apologized. I was shown that anyone can be touched by the presence of the Holy Spirit.

Many people will cry out to Jesus when this "Suddenly" happens, but others will not.

As his people find themselves in the presence and glory of the Lord, many will run from him out of fear and sin, just as the children of Israel did during the time of Moses. "And all the people saw the thundering, and the lightings, and the noise of the trumpet, and the mountain smoking: and when the people saw it, they removed, and stood afar off. And they said unto Moses, Speak thou with us, and we will hear: but let not God speak with us, lest we die. And Moses said unto the people, Fear not: for God is come to prove you, and that his fear may be before your faces, that ye sin not." (Exodus 20:18-20 KJV)

Christians that have compromised and adopted the world's standards of living will find themselves afraid of what is happening. Some will find themselves rejecting Jesus and turning their back on his mercy, because deep down they are aware of the sin in their life. Others will bring accusations against Jesus for allowing these trials and tribulations to touch their lives.

There is a scripture in the bible that says nothing shall separate us from the love of God which is in Christ Jesus our Lord. (Romans 8:39) The Lord is planning on removing the separation between himself and his people. As his children come to understand him and step into his presence, they will fall deeply in love with him. He will once again join himself completely to his betrothed, and they will know his love, forgiveness, and companionship.

Jesus went willingly to the cross because of his love for those that would someday belong to him. He allowed the soldiers to end his life so that those who accepted his sacrifice for sin would live with him for all eternity. "For God so loved the world, that he gave his only begotten Son, that whosoever believeth in him should not perish, but have everlasting life." (John 3:16 KJV)

When those that belong to Satan cry out for death; Jesus will give his people the will to cry out to live. Revelation 9:6 says, "And in those days shall men seek death, and shall not find it; and shall desire to die, and death shall flee from them." (KJV) Believers will find the Lord close to them, loving them, speaking to them, giving them the will to live and not die. Isaiah 55:3 says, "Incline your ear, and come unto me: hear, and your soul shall live; and I will make and everlasting covenant with you, even the sure mercies of David." (KJV)

Great faith that is needed to survive in the last days will be increased day by day as Jesus draws closer to his people.

It will not be done because they will ask him, it will be done because the Lord will establish it.

The word says that he that endures until the end will be saved. (Mark 13:13 KJV) The book of Revelation is often looked at as the revelation of disasters that are coming upon mankind in the last days. Yet the first words of the book say, "The Revelation of Jesus Christ, which God gave unto his servants." All the events that will take place, the Seals, the trumpet judgments, and the bowl judgments will remove the blinders from the world to the existence of their Savior, and Master.

Jesus' presence will be a living reality that surrounds his people. Like a women who lies her head upon her husband's breast and can hear the beating of his heart, that closeness and intimacy will be shared between the Lord and his people. Jesus desires to share that nearness and comfort with you as you tenderly embrace each another. Knowing Jesus is to love and worship him.

In Acts 17:23 KJV, it says "For as I passed by, and beheld your devotions, I found an alter with this inscription, TO THE UNKNOWN GOD. Whom therefore ye ignorantly worship, him I declare I unto you." That lack of a relationship with the Lord of not knowing who he is and who he represents will no longer exist. You will no longer worship someone you do not know, for Jesus will reveal himself to you. The knowledge of Jesus is not the same as knowing him personally. The revelation of Jesus Christ, his miracles, grace and glory will fill the earth during the end times.

This "Suddenly" event that will transform so many lives is like being born again under very traumatic circumstances. Once the process has started it cannot stop until its completion has been reached. Billions of people will be thrust into an unfamiliar world, and only the loving presence of the Father God can comfort them. He will carry his people through the most sorrowful time they can possibly imagine.

It is hard to imagine how anything good can come out of all the sorrow that will be experienced. Jesus revealed to me that as a baby is born it goes through much tribulation in the birth canal before it comes into the world. The resulting trauma of birth results in amnesia for the child, a complete severing from the life in the womb and birth event. So it will be like when your world ends and your new life begins. His word says, "that like as Christ was raised up from the dead by the glory of the Father, even so we also should walk in newness of life." (Romans 6:4 KJV) This new life you enter into will bring you into a greater intimacy with the Lord; healing, transition, and deliverance will be poured out; and the blessings Jesus has stored up for you since the very beginning of time will rain down upon you.

Satan in crucifying Jesus thought he stopped God's plan from happening, but the opposite was true. God's kingdom was established and the salvation of many was assured. Once again Satan will try to stop God's plan, but this will only set up the final victory and the salvation of millions. When you question why a loving God would allow this "Suddenly" to happen, know that he sees the end from the beginning. He knows the harvest that it will produce, for time will soon be no more.

A person's comfortable life will become a place unfamiliar and unfriendly. Only by being in the presence of Jesus will there be peace and deliverance from fear of the unknown.

CHAPTER 4

It's a Jungle out There

I was given a vision of the future where a person's comfortable life had been turned into a thick jungle environment that was hostile and unfamiliar. It had become a prison of despair for many. In this vision, people were moving into prison cages. The land was strange and unfamiliar; a place where people preyed on one other. The spirit of fear was unleashed and many were afraid to go out of their homes because it was not safe beyond their enclosed space. Their surroundings were cruel and unforgiving.

I saw bars for walls, windows and doors; a one room cage. Long vines thickly covered every bar. Vines represent family, city, entanglements, or snares. Walls can represent limitation, unbelief, defense, obstacles. What we see in the natural oftentimes represents what we feel in our hearts. People will feel trapped, alone, with no way out. People will be moved out of the safe and familiar because that will be their only option. Many people will be confronted with a spiritual death that will threaten to choke the life out of them. There will be nothing to cushion the blows, as one event after another happens; earthquakes, hurricanes, tidal waves, fires, divorce, death, sickness and disease, etc. The bible says, "Men's hearts failing them for fear, and for looking after those things which are coming on the earth; for the powers of heaven shall be shaken." (Luke 21:26 KJV)

Many will feel lost and adrift in a world that no longer cares, but the word says he is a very present help in trouble. (Psalm 46:1) The Lord does not abandon his people, he will help them.

Abandonment

"Thus sayeth the Lord. The spirit of abandonment will rise. Parents will abandon their children, children will abandon their parents, people will abandon one another, spouses will abandon one another, friends will abandon one another; but he Lord will not abandon his people. Malls and buildings will be abandoned; even cities or areas of cities will be abandoned. People will abandon their cultures. Politicians will abandon their people for political gain and power, and ethnic cleansing will rise; gangs against gangs, ethnic groups against ethnic groups. With resources shrinking, youth will abandon the aged. Wisdom will be abandon for gain. Churches will be abandoned. Christ will be turned away from."

Jesus also spoke to me and said, "I will deny the actions of those that do not belong to me. My glory I will not share with another. My glory is free to work according to my will; he will not work according to man's will."

There was a time I thought I knew what was best for me

and prayed for instant help, and instant deliverance out of desperate situations, but only the Lord truly knew what was best.

When my ex-husband abandoned and divorced me I had three little girls and was pregnant with my forth. During that time the Lord stood by me and poured out his grace and glory. I cried out to the Lord as despair and hurt filled my entire being. His miracles for me started before I had even married. God revealed himself to me when I was 16 years of age, for he knew what would happen to my life that I would be abandoned and destroyed. The Holy Spirit spoke these words to me just before I entered into my time of tribulation. He said, "How can anything good, happen out of anything so bad?" When God says it is bad, it is bad.

As I look back on the following 40 years, I see the miracles that God performed in my life as I surrendered every area of my life to him. How he would heal and deliver me, and the blessings he had stored up for me would be poured out upon me in my latter years. Job 42:12 (KJV) says, "So the Lord blessed the latter end of Job more than his beginning." We oftentimes want to run from what is best, from what the Lord's will is in our life. We want the easy way, the instant way, and make choices for what we think is instant success; but ultimately our choices end up long term disasters.

Look at the will of God in Jonah's life. He wanted to abandon the people of Nineveh to their sin and allow God to destroy them; but the Lord wanted to extend his mercy if the people would repent. When Jonah ran from God not wanting to preach repentance to the people, his environment changed and he was cast into the belly of the whale. After Jonah repented, the whale spit him out on the beach, Jonah then obeyed God and preached to the people and they repented. The mercy of God is so great that people will not understand why the Lord seems to tarry so that others might be saved.

The word says we enter into his kingdom through tribulations. Heaven has been described that we might know an expected end. That final environment will have no sorrow and no tears. The Lord is allowing circumstances to come into this world that will bring people to salvation and to remove the sin in their life so that they might enter into heaven and be with him for eternity.

CHAPTER 5

Awareness

Have you ever desired for God to reveal himself to you, to be in his presence just once, to be given knowledge of him, his greatness, his wisdom, to know who and what he really is. I experienced such an encounter with God at the age of 16. This was not something a person would seek out, or plan to happen; but the Lord God Almighty came into my room that night, and fear and respect for him would enter into my being.

It was a quiet, very cold, wintery evening and everyone in the house had just gone to bed. I had all kinds of blankets piled on me to keep warm. Out of the blue, as I was snuggled down half asleep, God began manifesting his presence to me. Instantly I became wide awake and my heart started beating fast with excitement as I lay in my bed. His presence began growing and his existence became stronger and stronger. He was letting me know he was there, he was real, and who he was. Immediately his tremendous love began to engulf and fill me. As his love continued to grow and grow, it felt like every atom in my body was literally going to explode into billions of infinitesimal pieces, and at the same time I knew that this overwhelming love was not even equal to one iota of his being. You couldn't measure his love.

Then as quickly as I felt his presence of love, I began to be aware of his knowledge, his wisdom, his greatness, his being. As he increased, I began to become smaller and smaller. I wasn't even equal to that of an ant, then I became literally as nothing and fear came upon me. I was shown that God is so vast the mind could not possibly comprehend him. He brought himself down to a level where mankind could interact with him. What little we do know of him in the bible is written at a level are minds and understanding can accept, but he is infinitely more than that. He is more than the word God implies. "I AM," is a better word to describe him.

As fear gripped me, I asked myself how such a God could be mindful of me who was nothing. How could he even be aware of my existence? God then began speaking to me. He shared that his word had been misinterpreted many times but that was OK because his mercy covered it, and he said people were like planets, some with elements missing in them. During his visitation he blessed my life with knowledge of himself and his creation. Psalm 25:14 (KJV) says, "The secret of the Lord is with them that fear him; and he will show them his covenant."

God didn't just reveal himself because one day he decided to say "Hi" to me. He planned it as a sign about future events that would take place in my life. I would not be able to comprehend what was going to happen in my life, nor be able to rise above it without his help. The partial amnesia I suffered as the result of extreme mental abuse by my ex-husband was going to take a miracle to overcome. There was going to be a cost that would be paid for my salvation as I laid my life down, but God would be there for me, loving me, holding me together, and covering me with his mercy. In the beginning of my time of tribulation, all my love and yearnings would cause me to seek out the Father God and have a relationship with him, just as multitudes of his people will soon be seeking him out.

Jesus witnessed to me and said that for a period of time he had sacrificed a relationship with me in order for me to have a close relationship with the Father God. I wept, for missing out on someone so very special. I always wondered why I was so close to the Father God, and began seeking Jesus. The Jewish people are seeking to know the Father God but will soon seek to know Jesus.

There is a time coming when a false religion will come forth. This religion will have a form of godliness but the personal relationship with Jesus will be missing. This is the key to this false religion. After my encounter with God it came to me that there was something missing, my relationship with Jesus had not yet been established. You can know all about Jesus, but not know him. In Matthew 7:22-23 (KJV) the word say, "Many will say to me in that day, Lord, Lord, have we not prophesied in thy name? and in thy name have cast out devils: and in thy name done many wonderful works? And then will I profess unto them, I never knew you." Knowledge can lead you to Jesus, but knowledge is not a relationship.

What kind of a bond have you established with the Lord? For me, I prayed and asked Jesus for a personal relationship with him, for closeness with him. I cried out, not to just have

Jesus in my mind, but to have him in my heart. He then answered my prayer and our relationship was established. Our bond with one another has become stronger and stronger throughout the years as we went through adversities together. He is here with me and I am never alone.

A couple of mornings ago, as I was relaxing and sitting in my favorite chair thinking about my family, I began crying from the very depth of my being. As tears were falling down my face and I was sobbing because my heart was breaking, the glory of God began falling upon me, first bringing me to repentance, then to absolute surrender to him in every area of my life. This was necessary in order for me to receive the words of knowledge that God was going to impart to me; and to receive this knowledge I had to empty myself of all that I am in order to receive of him. There is a lot of cleansing that takes place as you shed tears.

The Father God began speaking to me how very precious Jesus is to him, how deeply he loves him. That he loves everything about his son, his hair, his smile, every beat of his heart, every breath that he takes, and even the very twinkle in his son's eye is loved by God. Every step Jesus placed on the earth, every gesture he made, every tear he shed, every word spoken is treasured by God. Nothing is more precious to God than his only begotten son. Jesus meant everything to him and he sent him to die for our sins. It would have been much easier for God to die then to send his son to die for us.

Each one of us would gladly sacrifice our own life for that of our children, yet the Father God sent his son to die a merciless death on the cross for us. One of the reasons the Lord allows death to come into our life is to teach us what love is and to teach us how to love. Many in the days ahead will learn this lesson.

Everything made by the Lord is treasured by God, because it is created by his son. For those of you who have children, do you remember when your child brought home from school their handprint molded in clay, presented it to you, and how you treasured it. Jesus created the earth and everything in it, including man. Then man became loved by God, because Jesus out of his love formed everything for his Father. When you remove Jesus from his creation, you remove what is most precious to God. It only then exists and God's favor is not upon it.

All of creation began morning when Jesus was crucified and no longer walked upon the earth; the plants, animals, land, etc. The earth is dying as a result of this loss. Every step Jesus placed upon the earth was precious to the land. As more and more, man is refusing to acknowledge Jesus as the creator, changes are taking place in the earth, and God the Father no longer blesses his son's creation, because his only begotten son is not in it.

Nothing can replace Jesus in the Father's heart. I did not in actuality understand what a precious gift would enter into my being; my body, soul, spirit, mind, will and emotions, when I asked Jesus into all areas of my existence. In the beginning, I did not know how God the Father would see Jesus in me, and how this would cause him to treasure my existence.

The Father God is beginning to turn away from his Son's creation because Jesus is being removed. As God looks upon creation and no longer sees his precious son, his judgments start to pour out because of sin. Only the presence and blood of Jesus allows God to extend his mercy. You cannot separate the presence of Jesus from his blood sacrifice.

The Father shared with me that he sees many symbols on the earth that are pointing the way to his son being removed. As people and governments blindly try to stop others from finding their Savior by removing these symbols from the earth, such as the Ten Commandments, crosses, bibles from hotel rooms, manger scenes, etc.; the Father God will replace these symbols with signs in the heavens that will point the way to Jesus. That until the end of time God will direct the way to his mercy and grace. Jesus said, "And there shall be signs in the sun, and in the moon, and in the stars, and upon the earth distress of nations, with perplexity." (Luke 21:25 KJV)

Pray and ask God to reveal to you how precious his son is, and where he can be found. This knowledge and gift will totally transform your life and you will never be the same again. Let his preciousness become a part of your life. When the Father God looks upon you he sees Jesus dwelling within and he smiles upon you, and his forgiveness, love, mercy, and favor pours forth transforming you.

In The Zohar (Medieval Jewish Book of Wisdom) it states that, "In the sixth part of the sixth millennium, the gates of supernatural knowledge will open above along with the wellsprings of secular wisdom below. This will begin the process whereby the world will prepare to enter the seventh, Sabbath, millennium." Soon a great deal of the Lord's spiritual truths will be released to his people, to help them come to know him, and to fill them with faith and trust for the difficult days ahead. Is the knowledge of the bible going to increase but the personal relationship with Jesus going to be lost? Ask Jesus to secure your personal relationship with him first.

Sometimes we base our decisions on feelings, closing our self off to the warnings and admonitions of the Lord Jesus. We often deny the direction the Lord wants us to go because we do not acknowledge his authority over us. How can we surrender all our being to him if we do not know him? Jesus desires to bring us into a right relationship with him and the Father God.

We are all children in God's sight. Even as adults we are still children compared to him and his knowledge. He never loses sight of our needs; spiritual, financial, emotional, or physical. He knows right where we are at all times and he knows just what is needed so that we can spend eternity with him.

The Lord asks us to come out of the world, not to be joined to her or adopt her principles for if we did we would partake of her plagues. The Lord would sanctify his people and set them apart from the children of darkness. The bible says, "For where your treasure is, there is your heart also" (Matthew 6:21 KJV). People have replaced seeking Jesus, with seeking material gain on the earth, pursuing what the entertainment industry has to offer, looking for relationships outside the will of the Lord, seeking power in leadership, changing standards in their life to match the worlds standards, and turning their backs on the biblical principles God established to keep his people safe and provided for. How much longer will a Holy God withhold his wrath on a world that has turned their back on him?

CHAPTER 6

Challenges

The Lord spoke to me a couple of months ago and said, "Challenging times are coming." The word challenging means demanding, wearing, testing, difficult, tough, etc

Many will not understand the outpouring of the Lord's Holy Spirit that is to come, nor what will be needed to make it through these difficult times. Trust will be a big issue. It is like walking down a pathway in complete and utter darkness with a steep bottomless cliff located on one side of the path, and rocks and thorny bushes that can rip your flesh apart located on the other side. You find yourself completely blind and scared, and cannot see where you are going. Trusting in Jesus and having him become the center of your existence will be your only answer as he tenderly holds your hand and guides you his way.

Wars and rumors of wars, pestilence, earthquakes, and famine will all challenge God's people, but the Lord will bring his people through their time of trials.

After Israel sinned and God passed judgment upon Israel, the people were led as slaves to Babylon, under the reign of Nebuchadnezzar. Yet Daniel, Shadrach, Meshach, and Abednego remained faithful to the God of their fathers. (Daniel 3) They faced many deadly situations where they were delivered from death. So will it be during the time of this "Suddenly" event. Jesus has a plan for each one of his people and these plans were designed and mapped out before the foundation of the world. One of my favorite scripture is, "Trust in the Lord with all thine heart; and lean not unto thine own understanding. In all thine ways acknowledge him, and he shall direct thy path." (Proverbs 3:5-6 KJV)

During the time when Jesus walked upon the earth, many of the Pharisees and Scribes, or Learned Men, challenged who Jesus was, his teachings and his authority. In the days to come, as Jesus begins to pour out his spirit supernaturally upon his people, many of these same challenges will be faced. Visions and dreams will be dismissed, words the Lord speaks to his people will be rejected and misunderstood, teachings will be ignored, and miracles will be disregarded by people that lack faith. It will stab at the hearts of many to have these signs and miracles rejected by those close to them.

Jesus will bring forth each person's own uniqueness that lies deep within them but it will not be easy. One moment you were increasing in your spiritual gifts and growing as a child should, and the next moment your spiritual gifts were manifesting full strength. The normal steps of growing these talents throughout a longer period of time will have ended. It will be difficult to balance the spiritual with the natural at first. You will make mistakes as you operate in your anointing, but do not despair, the Lord's mercy will cover it.

The Lord will pour out his glory over you to help you

through this trying time. Blessings you never dreamed of will take place in your life. Desires you never knew were inside you will be achieved. A whole new world will open up for you, one you never knew before. Jesus will help you fulfill your God given potentials.

Just as the Israelites were blessed in Egypt and provided for as world-wide famine filled the earth for seven years, so will it be during this "Suddenly" event. Josephs will rise up all over the earth to help their families and friends survive. The Holy Spirit will move upon his people with an anointing that will shock the world. The Lord's will and glory will flow through his people releasing miracles on a daily basis. Everyone will have a place in his kingdom, but the laborers will be few.

Jesus is preparing a place for his people to survive as untold sorrow floods the earth. As I was sitting on my front porch one day worshiping and praising the Lord, the Holy Spirit witnessed to me that I needed to intercede and pray for this little valley that I live in; to pray that it would survive what is coming, and that the people here would be prepared. He then directed me to pray for the animals and plants in the area, and to pray that the Lord would send someone here who would be here for us in an emergency.

Pray and ask Jesus for wisdom and knowledge on how he wants you to prepare, for he alone knows what you will face in the future. Not every area or every person will face the same thing or have the same challenges. Ask Jesus to direct your prayers and help you to know what to pray for, and he will do just that. When you know you are praying according to his will, you will know without a doubt you have what you are asking for.

My favorite time with the Lord is early in the morning as I sit on my front porch drinking my first cup of hot coffee for the day. I watch as the sun just begins to light up the beautiful hillside in front of me. I talk with my Jesus, share with him, and ask him numerous questions.

I was sitting there a little while ago, when I looked off to my left and then to my right and I saw the glory of the Lord resting over this area. It looked like a shimmering invisible cloud. As I looked and saw his glory covering the land, the Holy Spirit spoke to me and said that what I was seeing was a miracle for this place. Miracles are residing in the places of refuge that are being prepared by the Lord for these last days.

Many, who have come here to this area in the Ozark Mountains, have testified to me they felt safe here, and were directed by God to come to this place. When I first moved here, the Lord spoke to me and said he had placed his angels all around my home and it would be a place of safety for me. There are many places of safety being set up by the Lord. My sister and her husband, who live in Marysville, Washington, live in a place where ministers of different faiths are being led by Jesus to gather together and unite. For it is known by these leaders that this Marysville/Arlington area will be a location of refuge in the last days. The Lord has also witnessed to me that a friend of mine living in Loveland, Colorado will be kept safe.

Jesus will make the call, as he announces his imminent return to his people. The journey will be difficult for many to make, and the body of Christ will go through many challenges, and feel the sufferings their Lord felt on the cross. His believers will embrace their Lord and surrender their lives and futures completely to him. He will open the spiritual eyes and remove deafness from his people, and people will get to know him. The brainwashing the enemy has inflicted upon many immature Christians will be instantly removed. Jesus is Lord of Lords, and King of Kings, and his power and glory will manifest itself all over the world with signs and wonders.

CHAPTER 7

Stars

When I was a child I use to ask the question, "Why God, do you allow all these bad things to happen." As I grew older I realized only a child would ask this question of him; one who didn't know him or have a close relationship with him. Many would say it's about free will; but it's about our trusting him, believing that he loves us, and trusting in his reasons for allowing events to happen even when he doesn't explain them. He knows the end from the beginning and each person he has created has an impact on this world.

Have you ever taken a good look at the stars and wondered about them? Abram was told by God to "Look now toward heaven, and tell the stars if thou be able to number them, and he said unto him. So shall thy seed be" (Genesis 15:5 KJV). Many people assume this means that the number of stars represents a vast number of people, but what if it means more than a number. What if it means that each star represents a person's destiny on earth and that God has a plan already mapped out for their existence? That each star is designed just for them to signify their existence in God's mighty plan for humanity? Sailors use to cross the oceans taking measurements by stars to map their course.

Just as Jesus has his star that the wise men followed (Matthew 2:22 KJV), the Lord revealed to me we all have a star created for us and named after us. When you look up into the sky at night your star is there in all its brilliance and majesty. God created the heavens and the earth in the very beginning with his spoken word. He knew from the foundation of the earth those who would be his, and he created your star and your destiny before he created you. Ephesians 1:4 says, "he hath chosen us in him before the foundation of the world." (KJV)

As I am writing this the Lord shared with me that just as he created the stars and some have fallen to the earth; their impact may it be small or large does change things. Many are questioning the twenty little ones from Sandy Hook elementary School killed in the school shooting at Newtown. Their lives though they were here only a short time on earth had a bigger impact than most others who have lived longer. Their stars shine brighter than most and they glitter the sky with God's majesty. When you look up into the sky search for the brightest stars and know that their light shines down on a grieving world that has lost hope in the sovereignty of God. Every man, woman, and child was created with a purpose just as the stars in the heaven have a purpose. These littlest and brightest of all stars will help guide people in the right direction towards heaven. The word says, "And they that be wise shall shine as the brightness of the firmament; and they that turn many to righteousness as the stars forever and ever" (Daniels 12:3 KJV).

The Father God has loved this world with all of his being. He has many children to save and rescue. There are many signs and wonders in the heavens coming soon. It breaks his heart to know so many are fearful of what's coming. He is mindful of each and everyone one of us and he hears our cries. Jesus wept for Jerusalem and after Lazarus died, when he saw Mary and the Jews which came with her weeping, he wept. Jesus is touched by everything that happens to us. Look up into the heavens and know that he is watching over you.

There are a lot of laws God set in motion to operate his spiritual kingdom, and the devil tries to twist them into something bad. He has a way of unconsciously setting up his kingdom without us even realizing it and causing people to commit sin against the Lord.

Many people are caught up in the worship of actors, actresses, rock stars, etc. Have you ever wondered why they are called "stars" and have their "stars" on the Hollywood Walk of Fame? Many people follow them and elevate them to a position of idol worship and power. Credence is given to the words they speak or sing, and they are being paid tribute when people go to their movies and concerts which blaspheme God, that promotes and glorifies sin.

By calling them "stars," are you not confessing into being their status in this world? Are you glorifying actors, actresses, rock stars, etc., elevating them to a place high above the earth? There is a difference between looking up into the heavens and seeing God's glory that lights man's way, and man lighting his own way. Stars are a symbol of God's design and handiwork and an outcome that is mapped out for each one of us.

While the children of Israel wandered in the wilderness

for 40 years they carried away the idols of Egypt and the "star gods" they had made (Amos 5:26 KJV). Many of the actors, actresses, and rock stars of today have been made by a public that idolizes them, and people carry them in their hearts. Jesus is the only one worthy of our worship and praise, he is the love of God's heart, and Jesus gave his life to set us free.

The Israelites went into captivity because of idol worship and came under bondage. Just as Jesus declared in his word that the heavens belong to him, he is going to start bringing down these idols as a sign to his people that he will not share his glory with another, and he is returning soon. In Obadiah 4 (KJV) the word says, "Though thou exalt thyself as the eagle, and though thou set thy nest among the stars, thence will I bring thee down, saith the Lord. "

Not only is the Lord going to cast down stars of idol worship, you are also going to witnesses actual stars falling to earth. Immediately after the tribulation of those days "shall the sun be darkened, and the moon shall not give her light, and the stars shall fall from heaven, and the powers of the heavens shall be shaken" (Matthew 24:29 KJV).

In Psalms 115:16 (KJV) it says, "The heaven, even the heavens, are the Lord's?" Just as God commanded light to come out of the darkness of heaven, those that belong to the Lord will light the way for others during this time of great darkness. The bible says to look up for your redemption draweth nigh (Luke 21:28).

Look up and see your star shining brightly against the moonlit sky as a reminder that he knew from the very beginning of time those who belonged to him. Why don't you ask him to point your star out to you? Ask him to show you his plan for your life, and to help you find it. Your star is meant to be followed by others, leading them to the Christ; just as the Star of Bethlehem pointed the way for the wise men, leading them to their King and Messiah.

CHAPTER 8

Time No More

We are quickly approaching the end of days when time will cease to exist. We regulate our lives by time, but there are so many more lessons to learn about it. Time is becoming a curse because so many people are living on borrow time not only in their finances but in their health. We assume that because we are living in it, it belongs to us, and that is not correct. Not even eternity will belong to us, but Jesus Christ will share his eternity with us for everything belongs to him.

The Holy Spirit spoke to me one morning as I was sitting on my front porch praising him and said, when I created the heavens and the earth most people see what I created, its plants, animals, man, etc, as the miracles that were created. But few recognize that the day itself was formed by me to OPERATE as a miracle. Each day that you are living in is a creative miracle that surrounds your life.

Genesis 1:3-5 (KJV) says, "And God said, 'Let there be light: and there was light. And God saw the light, that it was good: and God divided the light from the darkness. And God called the light Day, and the darkness he called Night. And the evening and the morning were the first day." He set in motion each day in existence to operate as a creative miracle to surrounds us. Each day that we live in is a blessing from him. God weaves everyone's day together according to his plans and purposes for each individual.

Definition of day means a specified period of time; and definition of time means it operates at continuous duration; yet God existed in eternity before time was created. Jesus is changing the perception of time. Time was created for man's period of existence on earth. Because of man's sin, time is becoming something that hurts man and is consuming him. It is also separating them from their shepherd, so Jesus is releasing knowledge and tearing down the wall between him and his people where time is concerned.

In Psalm 31:14-15 (KJV) David prayed to the Lord and said, "But I trusted in thee, O Lord: I said, Thou art my God. My times are in thy hand: deliver me from the hand of mine enemies, and from them that persecute me." Persecute means also to harass or hound. When this "Suddenly" event happens, many will find themselves in very difficult circumstances. David acknowledged that time belonged to the Lord. He put his trust in the Lord to handle the difficulties he was going through. The Lord's people will also acknowledge that time belongs to God.

Jesus knows that many of his people are now slaves to time because they have borrowed against it. People have charged on credit cards, taken out loans for vehicles or household items, and have gotten cash advances on paychecks, etc., placing many in debt and liability to the lender. Jesus is moving to set his people free. The scripture says to, "Owe no man anything, but to love one another. (Romans 13:8 KJV)

Time is an element designed by God that affects our life and it belongs to him. Jesus desires to set us free from the bondage of time. Galatians 4:9 says, "But now, after that ye have known God, or rather are known of God, how turn ye again to the weak and beggarly elements, whereunto ye desire again to be in bondage?"

It will not be long before this "Suddenly" happens. Know that for you time no longer exist and accept this premise. Ask Jesus to share his time with you so that you will no longer claim ownership of it. His timing is perfect and when he shares his time with you he will be standing right next to you because it literally belongs to him. His blessing is upon it; to protect, to make provision for, to allow or not allow things that are going to happen on the earth to come upon your life. The decision is his and his alone. If he allows you to go through something, he will be with you as you go through it. There is tremendous peace in knowing this. The word of the Lord says, " In thee O Lord, do I put my trust: let me never be put to confusion. Deliver me in thy righteousness, and cause me to escape: incline thine ear unto me, and save me" (Psalm 71:1-2 KJV).

Many of the spiritual keys of his kingdom will be given to his people, and miracles will become a common occurrence. One of the things Jesus had me to do to unleash miracles all around me was to literally give him things; time, memories, feelings, hurt, children, words, sentences, finances, health, my mind, etc. He also had me give to him my past and present. When I gave him my future, he spoke to me and said, "You can't give me something that you don't have."

Our future does not belong to us but to the Lord. It is in his safe keeping, and for him to decide what is to be. He loves

44

and cares for us all very much, and there is no place I would rather be than in his protection and care. Very soon many will come to understand there is no future only Jesus. To me the words Jesus and future are interchangeable; I am in Jesus and Jesus is the future.

Jesus witnessed to me recently that I no longer live in the past or future, but I live in the presence of him. The concept of time will change for everyone.

But time is all about love as well. The Holy Spirit's anointing came upon me one day and I was filled with tremendous love for the unsaved. I then prayed unto the Lord for him to accept one day of my life as a sacrifice to him. The bible says that, "there is a time to every purpose under the heaven", and "a time to cast away" (Ecclesiastes 3:1-8 KJV). I was willing to die one day earlier so he could use that one day to give to someone else, maybe by extending their life so that they would be saved. This is his response to me, "I will accept one day of your life, but I choose the day you are living in." So now he is renewing my day, regenerating one day from another. I understand and know I live in a creative miracle each day, and I thank him for it.

In Matthew 6:34 (KJV) the word says, "Take therefore no thought for the morrow; for the morrow shall take thought for the things of itself." We have trained ourselves to always think about tomorrow, but tomorrow may not be here. How many of you are willing to give up one day of your life to cast it away and let Jesus have it, as your gift to him? Pray and ask the Lord Jesus to share his time with you; that you may live in his creative miracle, treasuring each and every day that he grants to you.

Jesus plans to be close to his people and not separated from them. He will share his abundant knowledge to help them, as he holds them together with his love. Our Lord will remove the obstacles that would keep us from being able to enter into his kingdom, or that would produce stumbling blocks to grow faith. "But without faith it is impossible to please him." (Hebrews 11:6 KJV)

Many of his people will spiritually face severe challenges and difficulties when this "Suddenly" happens. They will have run out of time and will be thrust into a world they do not know, for their world will now be filled with danger, loss, and great pressure.

Sometimes a birth is difficult and sometimes a birth is easy. Many will be born into his kingdom when the time is right for them to come forth. To be born prematurely could cause many premature problems, and even death. The bible says there is a time for everything, a time to be born, a time to live, a time to die.

Thus sayeth the Lord, "Time belongs to the Lord and no other can claim ownership of it. I will no longer allow it. Changes are coming to remove my people from the entanglements of sin, the entanglements of their past and present, to remove my people from the hostility towards one another. I desire peace between my people, not strife, contentions, and fighting's. To survive the events that are coming, you will need unity."

Choices made now will determine the destiny of many later. Little minute decisions now could mean big freedoms and great faith later. That which has been proven, will be unproven.

CHAPTER 9

Famine

Very soon people are going to be given the choice of serving Jesus or serving the Anti-Christ, they will not be given the choice of serving both. The one they do choose they will embrace with all their heart. There will be no middle ground.

Many people today are getting caught up in the spirit of the anti-Christ and don't even realize it. In pursuit of money and pleasure, they have surrendered a part of themselves to this spirit of self. When this "Suddenly" happens, people will be shocked into the realization that their life is no longer their own that they have been sold into slavery and bondage just as Joseph was. In whatever position you find yourself, trust God.

Joseph remained faithful to the Lord during his time of slavery and imprisonment. While Joseph was imprisoned he was brought before Pharaoh to interpret a dream. He had the future revealed to him, that there would be a time of famine for seven years. You have already had the future revealed to you. It says in Matthew 24:7 (KJV), there will be famines before Jesus returns. Even now there are indications that severe famine is starting. The summer of 2012 was a time of prolonged drought in America, where over 60% of the land was considered under moderate drought conditions. California is currently experiencing severe drought conditions.

During the end of days, many people will be crying out for Jesus to feed them. Those that are hearing from the Lord are currently preparing for this food shortage. He does not want us to be afraid we will not have enough, for he has taught us he is our provider. Also, pray and ask the Lord what he would require of you to give to others. For me the answer has already been given, I am to give 10% of any food I might have to those that have none, and Jesus will bless the 90% that is left.

We need to love others and not be afraid to help them. I John 4:18 (KJV) says, "There is no fear in love; but perfect love casteth out fear: because fear hath torment. He that feareth is not made perfect in love."

Will I have everything I need during this time, I doubt it, so I am preparing spiritually, increasing my faith by reading of the exploits of others who have been supernaturally provided for during their time of great need. George Muller's book, "Answers to Prayer," where he established Orphan-Houses is a great book. It is about the feeding of a large number of orphans on faith when there was no food in the house. There is also Corrie Ten Boom's book, "The Hiding Place," a book about God's grace and glory that reigns down upon his people during their time of great need. Preparing spiritually is as important as preparing physically. Jesus says he will pour out his wrath on the children of disobedience (Colossians 3:6 KJV). We need to prepare our hearts for what is to come. This "Suddenly" event will have great consequences for people.

Do not become part of the great falling away where people

will be offended of Christ when they begin to suffer for his kingdom. The Lord has warned us so that we will not be caught unaware. He has given us a little time to prepare, but time is running out. He said to rejoice, for we know he is coming soon.

Jesus has watched over me all my life as I have gone through many tribulation type experiences. He has always been there and when I couldn't stand he carried me. Jesus proved himself to me time and time again as I lived in situations beyond my control. All of his children are precious in his sight and he will be there for them in their time of great need. Not one child of his will ever be abandoned. Hold tightly to the scripture that says, "I have been young, and now am old; yet have I not seen the righteous forsaken, nor his seed begging bread." (Psalm 37:25 KJV) His grace and glory is greater than any event or catastrophe that can take place in your life.

CHAPTER 10

Slavery and Bondage

In America greed, covetousness, and idolatry have taken over the people of this nation; but Jesus has a plan to set his people free. Most of America's citizens have now gone under bondage and slavery just as the Jewish people did when they lived in Egypt during the time of the Pharos. In the beginning the Israelites prospered and grew in strength, but after 400 years their lives became unbearable and they ended up with a very cruel taskmaster over them.

The people in America once a free people have also entered into their time of slavery. They have sold themselves into bond slaves by debt; and laws have been passed that limits their freedom. The Ten Commandments that God established to rule over his people have now been declared unconstitutional and the cross of Jesus is being removed that testifies of his mercy and forgiveness.

The Lord hears the cries coming from the very heart of his people, crying to be set free. The Lord is going to deliver his people from their sins and set them free to serve him. He is going to fill them with his righteousness and holiness because without it they won't see the Lord. Soon the Lord will strike America with great adversity, and with the plagues of Egypt to bring his people out of bondage. No longer will he allow them to serve other Gods and idols, for he is a jealous God. In Exodus 34:14 (KJV) it says, "For thou shalt worship 'no other gods; for the Lord, whos' name is *Jealous*, is a jealous God:"

Just as in Egypt, the sins of this nation have risen into the nostrils of the Lord. Instead of offering sacrifices to the Lord, sacrifices' are given to the idols of pleasure and greed. There were once sorcerers in Egypt practicing witchcraft, and now in this time and place, they cover this land from one end to the other. Do they think they can hide in darkness and the Lord will not know where they are?

Many signs have been given to this nation to repent. Just like the light in Egypt was blotted out so has the truth in this nation. False Gods have arisen that are an abomination to God. Just as God displayed his power by destroying the false Gods in Egypt, as surely as the Lord lives, he will also destroy the false Gods of this nation.

The children of Israel were forced to put their children to death in Egypt for population control because the rulers were afraid the Israelites would become stronger than they were. In our nation, we are putting our unborn to death by choice. Millions of our unborn has been sacrificed to the God of greed and lust. Many of the same plagues that struck Egypt will strike this world. Revelation 18:4 (KJV) says to come out of her, my people, that ye be not partakers of her sins, and that ye receive not of her plagues."

Has anyone ever considered what the unborn feel when they are aborted, especially those aborted during the last trimester when they would survive. These babies feel pain. They are instantly delivered upon their death into their heavenly fathers loving arms, but how much trauma did they go through before they died. Very soon our world will receive the reaping of this trauma. We will be delivered into the arms of trauma and pain, learning that God is sovereign after all. To those that repent and ask for forgiveness, his mercy will be poured out, and his comforting arms will surround them. He will wash away their tears and heal their wounds.

In 1620 the Pilgrims first sailed to America on the Mayflower in the hope of establishing a purified church and colony. The Mayflower blown off course landed at Cape Cod in Massachusetts outside the territory of the British. This frightened the pilgrims to be outside the protection of the British Crown, so they created and signed the Mayflower Compact. In the Mayflower Compact it stated that the colony would be "established for the Glory of God and advancements of the Christian faith," and it was signed "In the presence of God and one another," establishing a covenant with God. In this manner America was established as a Christian nation.

There are many people who stand before the Lord praising him and asking him to spare America to once again make her a Christian nation. Their cries have risen to the throne room of God and will not go unanswered. The Lord made a covenant with our forefathers. Even though many of the agreements have now been broken, God will move upon her people.

As I was waking up this morning the Lord began witnessing to me about adversity. How in II Chronicles 15, adversity was sent by the Lord to bring Israel back to the Lord during the time of Asa. His word says that, "Now for a long season Israel hath been without the true God, and without a teaching priest, and without the law. But when they in their trouble did turn unto the Lord God of Israel, and sought him, he was found of them. And nation was destroyed of nation, and city of city; for God did vex them with all adversity." (II Chronicles 15:3-4,6 KJV)

At this current time our nation has followed this same pattern by turning its back on God, rejecting his laws by banning the ten commandments from our courts, and forbidding prayer in schools. God in his mercy will once again pour out his adversity to bring our nation back to him. When Israel returned to their God with all of their heart, he forgave them.

One thing I have learned of the Lord is that when he gives me a word from him, I know it will come to pass. Very soon this "Suddenly" will take place. The Lord will decide the fate of each person in this nation, for he will have justice. Many hearts will be tried, and many will be chastised. For his words says, "For whom the Lord loveth he chasteneth, and scourgeth every son whom he receiveth. But if ye be without chastisement, then are ye bastards, and not sons." (Hebrews 12:6,8 KJV) Even now this time of trial and chastisement has already begun, but when it is over the presence of Jesus will surround his people. God's glory will fall upon his believers and they will do great and mighty things for their Lord. Jesus is going to set up his standard against the enemy.

When this "suddenly" happens great faith will be needed like David's. While everyone else in the army was shaking with great fear, David stood up in faith and slew the giant

Goliath in the valley of Elah. Great faith is coming to the Lord's people. Everything that hinders trust and confidence in Jesus will be stripped away; for the Lord is rising up a powerful army in these last days, one that will stand up in faith, in Jesus name.

The Holy Spirit witnessed to me that Billy Graham's final message to the United States on "My Hope for America" was prophetic in that it testifies God is going to bring this nation to the cross in order to save it as there will be no other way.

There is a circumcision coming to the hearts of the Lord's people. The spiritual sufferings the Jewish people felt will be placed upon the Gentiles for they will know their Jewish God and Savior, for he is the same over all. His people will become holy unto the Lord. His Saints will bring praises before the Holy One of Israel and creator of all. There will be worship and praise as the Lord's holiness enters into his people. Hereafter angels will be ascending and descending upon his people. Do not be afraid of what is coming for the Lord of Glory will be with you, and he is mightier than all. All of heaven has waited for this day, so rejoice for your salvation draws near.

As America is brought before the Lord for her sins, there is hope that Jesus will not completely destroy this nation. That he will save America and return this nation to him. It has been prophesied by many that revival will sweep this nation. In 1993 there was a prophecy given to Dr. David Yongii Cho about America, when he asked the Lord if he had forgotten America. The Lord's answer was that he had not forgotten America, that he would pour out his Spirit before his coming, and that the glory of God would fall on its people.

This prophecy does not mean that we would escape all of the judgments about to be poured out upon this nation. It was the pouring out of God's judgments upon Egypt that brought his people out from under the bondage and slavery of Egypt during the time of Moses.

Jesus shared with me that one of his last warnings, to be given before his return, will be our fleeing into life boats. Being in a life boat means you will be floating along, not being able to move in the direction you want, compressed about by the elements, and having limited resources. It will be a time of great patience. You will be waiting, praying, and hoping that you will survive until the Lord comes; seeing that there will be no way out of the situation you will find yourself in. You will need divine intervention by Jesus to rescue you.

CHAPTER 11

Words from the Lord on Obedience

The anti Christ has a captive audience, and he has been setting up traps and entanglements for a long time. Most people do not like the answers they get from the Lord so they seek answers elsewhere. The Holy Spirit spoke to me recently and this is what he said.

"Many speculate on what each seal judgment represents, but until it actually happens many can only guess about what these events are, and how they will affect a person's life. I pass knowledge unto my servants to obey me in certain areas. If they do, I know they will be spared from certain judgments, but if they do not obey me then they face those judgments. I instructed Abraham to offer his son on the alter as a sacrifice to me. He did not know what the plan was that I had prepared if he was obedient.

When the children of Israel went into the promised-land they knew they were to conquer the land, but did not know what they would face, or how it was to be done until the time. So will it be with the challenges and difficulties you will face. Trust and confidence in me will be most important. Seek these two things; ask for trust and confidence to come into your life. It will help you through the days ahead. You can ask Jesus anything and he will answer you, but sometimes the answer hurts and you may not want to listen. Those who serve me are not paying lip service to me will need to obey me even if it hurts. The solution to a problem I might give you could be that you move away from your family to a different state. What if your family turns from you? What if I instruct you never to talk to your best friend even if that person is spirit filled and has a might anointing from me? Will you reject what I am saying, not believing the words are coming from me, not believing the truth of my words.

I spoke to Adam and Eve not to eat the forbidden fruit, but they chose not to believe me. They were as close to me as a person can be, yet they chose to believe a lie. Once again Satan is coming with a lie that will deceive many. Those that have surrendered completely and totally to me in every area will not be deceived. Those that are not obeying me, those that are not mine will not hear my voice. You cannot live in both worlds. The choice is yours. I know those that give me lip service. I know those that serve me from the heart.

What is the greater good? This question will be presented to you. Do not be deceived by this question. Will you try to preserve your life or give your life to me? Will you allow me to decide if you will live or die? My children are so afraid of the spirit of death. Do not misinterpret what I am saying. What is the spirit of death? How will it operate in the last days? What will my glory reveal to you? Who will be my Jonah, who will be my Joshua, who will be my Gideon in the last days? Did they not defeat the spirit of death?

I have made many covenants with many people. Who has kept covenant with me? Did Job question me? Do you question me? I sent my son to the cross so you would have answers, but many of you are going to the cross, why? Thus sayeth the Lord."

Many may ask why the Father God speaks to me. When a person accepts Jesus into their heart the Lord begins to do a work in their life. He knows the deepest needs that are coming from a person's heart. My deepest need was to have a relationship with the Father God, so Jesus sacrificed his relationship with me. Jesus was there and I had many visions of him, but the majority of my time I was allowed into the presence of the Father. Jesus was obedient to the Father's request that he bring me into Father's presence so I might be used in the last days to help his people.

I was taught that when you surrender to the Lord you are covered by his blood and mercy. The areas you have not surrendered to the Lord, those areas then are under the law, and he deals with us according to his will. He often withholds judgment for a very long time, giving a person time for repentance. But time is now being shortened. Jesus is cleaning up his bride before his return. That is why it is very important to give all that you are to the Lord; the good, the bad, and the ugly. He can then go into those areas and give you grace to overcome the areas you can't, and he will change a person's heart according to his will and timing. When you are weak, then he is strong if you obey him.

Many will justify their actions; exalt them self instead of the Lord. The Tower of Babel fell because man exalted himself, so God changed their environment by confusing their language. Man had an opinion of himself that was wrong. Man united against the Lord lifting himself up. He thought he was as good or equal to God.

The Holy Spirit has witnessed to me that many sacrifices' will take place in the days ahead in order to survive. You will have to give up many things. When you read the Old Testament and see all the numerous animal sacrifices, these animals were to be unblemished, perfect in every way before they could be given to God. No longer will he accept defilement and blemished gifts. No longer will he accept sin offerings in a person's life. He wants a spotless bride one without blemish.

Many who give their life to the Lord believe they can go on sinning. The Lord will not allow this to continue. You cannot serve two masters. For those that seek him, he will extend his mercy and grace to help them remove the sin in their life. Just like the animal sacrifices were to be spotless he wants those who serve him to be spotless. He will cover his people with his blood as he removes the sin. But if his people refuse to remove the sin, he will cast them out of his presence. He will no longer accept lip service.

Man thinks mind over matter is the answer, but it is his word that reveals man's heart and changes him. Man is incapable of changing himself. People try and try to stop sinning, but they fail to heed his word. Only the acceptance of Jesus into the heart of man will change him. The word says, "Greater is he that is in you, than he that is in the world." (I John 4:4 KJV)

"Greater love hath no man than this, that a man lay down his life for his friends." (John 15:13 KJV) The Israelites were taken into captivity to Babylon because of sin and hardness of heart. They went into a totally different culture and environment. People are becoming harsh and unforgiving, sending many of into bondage. Love is being lost. No long are the Lord's children willing to sacrifice them self for others. Their environment is going to change.

CHAPTER 12

Charges, Charges, Charges

One of the most astonishing words the Lord gave to me was, *"Charges, Charges, Charges."* These are the recent words the Lord has given to me that will come from his people. Many of the Lord's people are soon to bring charges against the Lord for his failure to act on their behalf before his return. Just as Satan presents charges against the Lord's people, many will bring charges against the Lord. Many will not understand the work the Lord is going to do on their behalf by allowing these events to happen in their life. That he needs to separate them from this world in order from them to enter into his kingdom. The bible says in Acts 14:22, "we must through much tribulation enter into the kingdom of God." (KJV)

Just as Satan is going to be thrown out of heaven and the accusations being brought against the Lord's people will stop. The Children of God need to be careful so they do not bring charges against their Lord and the same thing happens to them. They would find themselves no longer having access to their Lord and he no longer is hears their cries. Not only will people bring charges against their Lord, but this reflects a bigger problem, rebellion; for his people are charging on their charge cards and feel guilt building up inside them as the Holy Spirit witnesses to them to stop. He is going to put a stop to this practice for rebellion is as witchcraft.

The word says in I Corinthians 13:12(KJV), "For now we see though a glass, darkly; but then face to face; now I know in part; but then shall I know even as also I am known." As Christians are shaken with circumstances beyond their control, the Lord's people will call out to Jesus to save them. Do you remember when Jesus wept over Jerusalem because he knew it would be destroyed, he also is weeping over his people today knowing the destructions they are going to face. I see a vision of Jesus holding a tiny little baby wrapped in a receiving blanket, and Jesus is weeping because he knows what this child is going to face because there is no other way. In a short period of time, his people will face much sorrow and it brings him to tears for his people.

Jesus had me do two things; give up bacon replacing it with turkey bacon and he asked me to eat garlic. One year after being obedient to the Lord he shared with me what it represented as a sign to others. He shared with me that the giving up of bacon testified against others that they were living "high off the hog," and eating garlic testified against man that others thought they were immune against what is coming and they are not immune. Also in being obedient to the Lord he would bless my life in two areas, being a better money manager, and he would bless my health with a better immune system. The Lord is going to ask his people for obedience.

CHAPTER 13

Changing the Environment

"Thus sayeth the Lord. The spirit of abandonment will rise. Parents will abandon their children, children will abandon their parents, people will abandon one another, spouses will abandon one another, friends will abandon one another; but he Lord will not abandon his people. Malls and buildings will be abandoned; maybe even cities or areas of cities will be abandoned. People will abandon their cultures. Politicians will abandon their people for political gain and power, and ethnic cleansing will rise; gangs against gangs, ethnic groups against ethnic groups. With resources shrinking, youth will abandon the aged. Wisdom will abandon for gain. That which has been proven, will be unproven. Churches will be abandoned. Christ will be abandoned.

I will deny the actions of those that do not belong to me. My glory I will not share with another. My glory is free to work according to my will; he will not work according to man's will."

People will have to face their fears. When God came down to talk with Moses on the mountain, the environment

63

changed; there were clouds. Look at all the plagues the Egyptians went through, it changed their environment. The Israelites walked on dry land through the red sea. The waters divided and the environment was changed. Jesus rebuked the waves when there was a storm. The storm was an environment that caused fear and Jesus healed the environment and brought peace and calm. Jesus showed the apostles how to walk in the miraculous when he walked on the water. Peter tried, but because of loss of faith he sank, then Jesus rescued him.

Jesus said before his return the mountains would shake and be cast down. Just before the Lord's return when Israel faces her greatest peril, Jesus will stand on the mountain in Israel and the mountain will split in two, allowing the Israelites to escape through the mountain when they are attacked and flee to Petra.

Look at Jonah. When he ran from God his environment changed and he landed in the belly of the whale. Then look at Jonah after he preached to Nineveh and he hid under the gourd from the sunshine and the gourd withered so the sun beat down on him. Jesus rebuked the fig tree and it withered and died because there was no fruit. Noah went through the flood because the Lord changed the environment to stop the sin. The word says the days shall be shortened or no man would be saved. Once again the Lord will change the environment.

In the last days Woodworm falls and the drinking waters become bitter and large numbers of mankind will die. Earthquakes and storms will take place as the environment turns against man for sin. John the Baptist was put in prison and was then beheaded. His environment was changed. The

Apostles were put in prison many times and rescued from the hostile environment. Heaven has been described. That final environment will have no sorrow and no tears. Many have died and returned from the dead to testify of heaven's beauty.

Sometimes a birth is difficult and sometimes a birth is easy. Many will be born into his kingdom when the time is right for them to come forth. To be born prematurely could cause many premature problems, and even death. The bible says there is a time for everything, a time to be born, a time to live, a time to die. Thus sayeth the Lord, "Time belongs to the Lord and no other can claim ownership of it. I will no longer allow it. Changes are coming to remove my people from the entanglements of sin, the entanglements of their past and present, to remove my people from the hostility towards one another. I desire peace between my people, not strife, contentions, and fighting's. To survive the events that are coming, you will need unity."

CHAPTER 14

Exploring Other Worlds

Your world is going to change. Jesus faced the temptation of being given the world. He refused it so that he could give us his world. This world belongs to Jesus. He defeated Satan at the Cross. Sometimes we see God outside of what he created but all of creation exists within him. Jesus essence is in everything he created, the universe and this world. Jesus is in everything. Our universe and our world exist within him. Oftentimes we focus on our world instead of his kingdom. Jesus gave up heaven to teach us of his kingdom. Jesus exists in many planets, in many forms, but here in this world we were created in his image.

Salvation comes in many ways and in many forms. Buy this I mean we all go through different experiences that lead us to Christ, and we all live in different worlds where our cultures, heritage and patterns that surround us are different. Oftentimes our worlds collide, and we establish a life compatible and agreeable with each other. Marriage is often a combining of different cultures, different likes and dislikes different attitudes and beliefs.

Jesus learned to live in both worlds, his kingdom and the natural and he made provision for both. He saw the collision between different cultures, faiths, and what would happen if they did not live in agreement with one another. He knew what would happen if one refused to co exists with one another. He knew what the joining of two worlds would need.

People are exploring one another's world all the time, and often find they are not compatible and cannot exist with one another. Sometimes they find the world hostile and destructive to them. People on the fringe of society oftentimes cannot exist with others because of their beliefs. Once people remove themselves from their own world and go to another world they cannot oftentimes get back to their original state. Sometimes they are alive but live in neither world.

People who cannot live in their own world, how can they adapt and live in a different world. Jesus knew who he was, where he came from, and where he was going. His temporary journey here on earth did not change the perception of who he was. But he did adapt to his temporary abode. Jesus did not take any risks, he knew exact ally how he was to live, who he was to live for, and he knew the truth about the world around him. He did not let himself get deceived. He did not join himself to the world he found himself in.

Jesus knew what this world would turn itself into and he came with an invitation for those who lived on planet earth to come to his world. But there were conditions that needed to be met in order to enter into his world. People cannot force their way to his world, they cannot use words to convince him for he knows their heart whether they are giving lip service to him. Jesus knew the condition of man's heart. He only wanted those that would bless his world, not curse his world; but mankind needed to change his heart in order to be a blessing to his world. There is only one way to become a blessing, only one way to change a person's heart.

Changes are coming to man's environment and many will want to escape. Many will turn to drugs, some to sex, some to anything that will take the pain, despair, and suffering away. Jesus offers a way into his world. Jesus already paid the cost. All a person has to do is accept who he is, where he is from, and invite him into their life to receive of him his pardon, and for him to remove the sin within. His word says, " For God so loved the world, that he gave his only begotten Son, that whosoever believeth in him should not perish, but have everlasting life. For God sent not his Son into the world to condemn the world; but that the world through him might be saved." (John 3:16-17 KJV)

CHAPTER 15

Alignment

At times your environment will be blistering hot and frigidly cold in places. It will be almost impossible to live at times without divine guidance and help from the savior, Jesus Christ. It is like everything is out of alignment with the universe. People's lives will be out of alignment with one another. Your world will be out of alignment with other worlds. Reality will collide with fantasy as events are taking place in the earth.

The power of prayer will set many things right in your world; will bring many aspects of your life into alignment with your creator. Jesus created the heavens and the earth with his spoken word. He set the planets in alignment with one another. The Father God revealed to me that we are like planets some with elements missing in them. He designed each person to fit into the proper place in his universe.

The Father God spoke to me and said, "I have allowed many trials and testing's to come upon my children that have hurt them deeply. My will was not to judge them or to hurt them but to try their hearts. Many will come to me asking for mercy in the days to come as tribulation times come upon them. My answer to my children will be; when did you give me mercy, why did you not ask me to help you forgive them, to help you have mercy for your enemies and to bless them? Many will want to come home but I will say it is not time yet. First you need to know my will, then you need my will in your life, then you must follow my will and accept my will. For better or worse; for richer or poorer; in sickness and in health my people make vows. Are they certain they can keep them? What happens when they break a vow? Do I break my vows? Do they ask for my help with keeping them, or not keeping them? Ask and you shall receive. His voice or my voice; whose voice are you listening to. What does my voice sound like? Do you ask to hear my voice? The word says I will show you great and mighty things which you knoweth not. I will be known of you before the great day comes.

Give me your mercy and accept my mercy; whose is greater? Greater love hath no man than he lay his life down for his friend. He who is friends with me is an enemy of the evil one, and the evil one cannot touch him unless I allow it. First blood moon of the tetrad is a sign to the believer of God's mercy; that the blood of Jesus is over you. Nothing shall separate you from the love of God which is in Christ Jesus our Lord. To the unbeliever it is a sign of what is to come."

When I started writing this book I asked the Lord to give me answers for what is to come. I did not just want to know what is coming. I needed to understand the why. He shared so many things with me.

CHAPTER 16

Obedience

The Lord is separating the sheep from the goats. He is going to manifest his supernatural and divine intervention into the lives of his people as he pours out his mercy upon them. He knows those who truly belong to him and those who are only giving him lip service, whose heart is far from him. Some of his children are not aware that he is there. Me, I need that assurance that he is there. I cry out for it. I need that closeness and relationship with him. It means everything to me, he is everything to me. The word says nothing is powerful enough to separate us from the love of God.

I will share a personal word for me the Father God gave me. "It breaks my heart knowing you care for me, that you love me so much, and would give your life for me as my son did. Each day is a complete miracle of events designed just by the Lord to bring us together. I love you. The trauma and pain the world must suffer is a part of my love. Without it, many will not know me, or know the reality of my presence. Comfort yourself with these words, The King is coming soon. Jesus chooses those who will serve me. My son is a reflection of me. His words are a reflection of me. His walk on the earth was to manifest my glory.

What is the purest form of love, self-sacrifice. Jesus manifested this love on the earth. No matter what man did to him, no matter how they acted towards him, he sacrificed his life for them on the cross and forgave them. His trust in me brought him into my presence. His obedience to me was rewarded. His faithfulness was rewarded. Truth has its reward. Speak the truth. I will share with you many words of truth. These revelations will turn many hearts to their Lord. As you have remained faithful to Jesus, he will always be faithful to you, and you will be rewarded. My desire for you is to know me. Comfort yourself with these words. The truths I have given to you will bless you, your family, and a multitude of others. Miracles are a daily occurrence in your life. My time is precious and I have time for you. You share with me and I share with you. Jesus is a rewarder of those that diligently seek him.

I will fan the embers that have been left unattended. They will ignite into an inferno. The embers have been fanned. Montgomery, Little Rock, Pasadena, Tulsa, Corpus Christi, Mount Sinai, my glory shall ignite a fire from within. The hearts and minds of my people will change. They only see a glimmer now. Thus sayeth the Lord."

I did not share these words with you to speak of myself, but to speak of my Lord and Savior Jesus. To share with you the love the Father God has for mankind. I am nothing compared to him and his glory. I have sinned and have been chastised mightily. I John 1: 8-10 (KJV) says, "If we say that we have no sin, we deceive ourselves, and the truth is not in us. If we confess our sins, he is faithful and just to forgive us our sings, and to cleanse us from all unrighteousness. If we say that we have not sinned, we make him a liar, and his word is not in us." Paul says in II Corinthians 12, "though I be nothing."

When Adam and Eve disobeyed God, sin entered into man. Jesus came to remove the sin. God is obedient to his word. We are all obedient to someone. If a person were to choose between obedience and love, which would he choose? Which is greater? A husband must be obedient to God, and a wife obedient to her husband in the Lord. A husband stands between her and God. Jesus stands between be us and God. Eve sinned first. Adam knowing God and the judgment that would follow sinned for Eve covering his wife. He sacrificed his life out of love for her, facing the same judgment. Married couples go through the same judgment together. I believe sometimes the sin is so great in one spouse God allows them to separate so that the same judgment does not fall on both. Only God can make a way when there is no way. Sometimes a small act of disobedience can lead to great destruction. Like Eve eating the apple. The simple act caused sin to enter in to all areas, so man had to die. I believe the key to marriage is finding an obedient man to God, to his word, and to Jesus.

Greed

John 2:13-16 says, "And the Jews Passover was at hand, and Jesus went up to Jerusalem, And found in the temple those that sold oxen and sheep and doves, and the changes of money sitting: And when he had made a scourge of small cords, he drove them all out of the temple, and the sheep, and the oxen; and poured out the changers' money, and overthrew the tables; And said unto them that sold doves, Take these things hence; make not my Father's house an house of merchandise." We are the temple of the Holy Spirit and many have allowed greed and covetousness to enter into their being. Jesus is not going to allow the greed and covetousness that has entered into his people to continue. He is going to act against his people to deliver them from defiling his temple. Overturning the tables was done in a dramatic fashion.

There is a "Suddenly" event that is very soon going to take place; that will astound his people. He is going to cleanse his people from their filthiness. Many only see the merciful Lamb of God, and do not respect who his truly is. The word says to not fear the one who can kill the body, but fear the one who can kill the soul and steal your salvation. Many fear the anti-Christ more than Jesus. Fear and respect for Jesus will come into a person's being. The word says fear is the beginning of wisdom. Sometimes being in the Lord's presence is to quake with fear and fall at his feet like a dead man. Look at the Apostle John and others. Revelation 1:17 (KJV) says, And when I saw him, I fell at his feet as dead. And he laid his right hand upon me, saying unto me, Fear not; I am the first and the last."

CHAPTER 17

Perceptions

Perceptions of who we are have diminished over time. Our awareness of and our understanding of ourselves, people, situations, etc, has lessened. People in the United States have a false sense of reality. This makes them particularly susceptible to the anti-Christ. An awareness and understanding of who we are in the Lord will open the eyes and ears of his people. As false securities are taken away, a new perception will arise for the Lord's people. I have a feeling those that belong to the anti-Christ will get their perceptions from him; the blind leading the blind. Television has become a tool used by the enemy. People no longer filter out the truth of any given situation. Their perceptions are being weakened and great brainwashing has begun. Just as people no longer exercise their body, they no longer exercise their ability to perceive, to discern situations, to discern the truth of any given situation. Why are we here? Why have we been placed on the earth? Why were we created? Why is Israel resurrecting a dead language, if not to testify of God's truth? The Jewish people once again are being used by the Lord to show God's truth, to bring awareness and growth into our perceptions, to testify of it. Watch Israel as she is a sign to the world about perceptions, about who we are in the Lord.

An awakening has begun. As people become aware of whom they are in the Lord the enemy will be stopped from using the Lord's people for his own messages. This will infuriate him causing him to strategize against the Lord's people to destroy them. Greater love hath no man than he lay down his life for Jesus and their friend. Friendship with Jesus will cause separation from the world.

Instead of people loving the world, they will love their Lord and Savior, Jesus. The awakening that is coming is different. Bitterness is coming to the world, separation is manifesting itself, and judgment will join them. But those of the Lord's people will love others, and love themselves. They will forgive others and forgive themselves. The Lord's people will be made whole. They will not be joined to others, or see other parts of themselves used by Satan. In the bible it talks about cutting off the hand, or removing the eye if it offends. Satan used his body parts and puts them on the Lord's people. The Lord is removing those parts and making his people whole and one with him. Never again will his people be joined to others, or joined to false Gods, or idols.

One day the Holy Spirit spoke to me and said, "The wicked will eventually be removed from the earth, and the Lord's people will inherit everything. This is promised in his word. The Lord promised many things throughout generations. Generational blessings and promises will be restored to this people. People look to the here and now, and are short sighted. The Lord is healing that perception. Goals and values will change. Perceptions about the Lord will be changed. My truth will be written in the hearts and minds of my people. My love for them is unconditional, yes unconditional. Many will learn this. Truth will come from my lips. Truth will be spoken from my lips.

God is not a figment of your reality. My reality will manifest to my people as great changes take place in the earth. Tornadoes, destructive elements will shake the world as my glory descends. Did not thunder and lightning descent when I descended and spoke to my servant Moses on my mountain? Did not the earth tremble as it is now? As my glory descends and my presence descends will not these things happen? Do not be afraid of me as the children of Israel were when I stood upon the mountain Was it not foretold that when I step upon the mountain of Israel the mountain will split in two. The closer I get to the earth, the more it shakes, the more lightning and thunder manifests itself. My glory has power, my glory is not weak, and my glory overshadows you. Changes are coming to the earth and to my people. As people learn who they are in me, you will shake the earth; you will cause signs and wonders to happen, lightening to pour forth from you.

Camels store water for long periods of time before they are given drink again. Store water; store the water of my word. Shortages of water are coming. Prepare for water shortages. Builders rejected my counsel. Now they will find their buildings will come down. Learn of me, learn to hear my voice. Exercise your perceptions. Exercise your body. I am coming soon to meet my glorious bride. Some take exception to me, to my word. Blast, Blast, Blast." (I have a feeling there will not only be explosions in the earth, by Jesus will blast his people out of their self-contained small world. He is going to move people outside their comfort zones.) "I will point my way to my people. Will you follow your way or my way? Will you choose your way or my way? The earth trembles at my glory. Are you stronger than the earth? Changes are coming. Changes are coming. Thus sayeth the Lord of hosts, the Lord of Glory, and the Lord of many."

CHAPTER 18

Words That Stand the Test of Time

Knowing who you are in the Lord is very important. Most every day I say affirmations out loud confirming who I am in the Lord. I was blessed by the Lord to know what happens when a person verbalizes declarations based on scripture. I was taught and given three divine appointments by Jesus over a period of twenty years to understand this gift of knowledge. One of the three aspects of this teaching was a dream showing its effect.

Many years ago I bought a book called, "Prayers That Avail Much, published by Word Ministries." It is a collection of scriptural prayers that covers all different kinds of areas; wisdom, salvation, healing, deliverance, oppression, women or men searching for a mate, children, finances, etc. I selected several prayers that I would say out loud as I sat in my car during lunchtime at work. I especially selected those on deliverance and healing.

On this one particular warm summer day, I was sitting in my car with the windows rolled down, when a heavenly atmosphere suddenly enveloped me. I was aware, heard, and felt all the angelic activity that was taking place in the spiritual realm around me as I quoted scriptural prayers out loud. There were not just a couple of angels but a multitude of angels working on my behalf as I was speaking. This opening of my spiritual eyes and ears greatly encouraged me to continue this routine daily, praising and exalting the Lord.

Then I was blessed with a second experience twenty years later. I was saying affirmations out of the back of a book called, "Commanding Your Morning," by Cindy Trimm. She had been a guest speaker on "It's Supernatural," and had given her testimony about how quoting scripture and saying positive declarations out loud from the bible had changed her life.

She and her family had lived in absolute poverty in Bermuda with no hope for a future; and she testified how her life, the lives of her family members, and others had totally changed after they began quoting words of faith out loud.

So following her example, I started speaking affirmations listed in the back of her book. After confessing these words of faith daily for a period of about six months, I once again had my spiritual eyes and ears opened. My bedroom where I had been quoting affirmations was filled with a large company of angels. I could hear the rustling of their garments as they moved. Then Jesus was standing in the midst of them. All of a sudden Jesus began speaking to them, commanding them to bring in the harvest that I had planted by speaking positive declarations out loud.

Jesus so tremendously blessed my life for being obedient to his word. "And whatsoever we ask, we receive of him, because we keep his commandments, and do those things that are pleasing in his sight." KJV)

Following this second encounter, I decided to retire early from my job, and move to a new state. For the first time in my life I bought my very own home, an A-frame cabin that I had been confessing for. A miracle was given to me to be able to buy this home.

You don't just confess the word once; you need to be diligent about it. Following this second eye-opener revelation, I received a third substantiation from the Lord concerning the speaking of words out loud, but this time it was in the form of a vivid dream.

I had been living in Missouri only a few months when I was given a dream from the Lord on how confessing the word out loud was changing my life. It was just before dawn when I began dreaming. In the dream I saw myself standing in a rather small inexpensive motel. I then left the motel and began walking towards a large historic landmark hotel that was located a few blocks away. I entered this hotel and began walking around noticing major construction happening all around me.

Everywhere I went there were extensive renovations going on; in the entry, main lobby, the dining room, the hallways, lounge, etc. There were torn out walls and new framing constructions being put up. I saw large and small tools laying everywhere, debris on the floor, workers hammering and sawing on different materials, and places so filled with construction it was difficult to saunter through. I noticed some lights not working in a few dimly lit areas where construction was taking place, and some rooms were inaccessible or unusable, etc. It looked like a total renovation of this remarkable hotel was occurring.

I was then shown to a hotel room by a female angel where two very exquisite changes of clothing, that could only have been designed by the Lord were given to me; one was a two-piece brilliant turquoise dress, and the other outfit was a beautiful pant suit. This angel asked me what outfit I wanted to ware; I chose the dress. The pant suit was then placed in a suit case so that I could take it with me for later. I then understood that all the construction that had gone on around me was the results of the words coming out of my mouth, and the two outfits represented two changes that were going to take place in my life.

God spoke into existence the creation of the heaven and the earth. Words are powerful and can create life or death.

The word says, "Bless the Lord, O my soul, and forget not all his benefits." (Psalm 103:2 KJV) There are benefits to speaking his words out loud; and death and life are in the power of the tongue.

Bible Is Alive

John 1:14 states, "And the Word was made flesh, and dwelt among us, and we beheld his glory." Jesus is alive today, and his word is alive and full of miracles. The Lord shared with me that when you read the bible it ministers to different areas of your life to set you free, bless you, and prepare you for the future.

The Old Testament ministers life to your past, removing the death and destruction that has entered into your being; and it brings healing, blessings, and deliverance into those areas where wounds and curses have existed since before you were born. It also sets you free from the past.

When you read the gospels, present tense, when Jesus was alive on the earth, the word of God ministers to your life, concerns, and cares that you are going through today.

When you read Revelation, or one of the prophets, it prepares you for the future. It starts changing your life today to meet the needs you will have then, and to remove and work out situations before they can occur.

His words are not dead words they are miraculous words, full of his grace, power, mercy, and glory. Even if you don't feel it, his words minister to you creating miracles to bless your life. The Bible blessed my life abundantly bringing me much needed healing and deliverance from the past, carrying me through my present, and creating for me a wonderful and safe future.

I always try to read my Bible, at least a couple of pages every night before I go to bed. I tell myself that if I really loved the Lord, I would want to spend time with him. What I desire to do before I sleep is to be extra close to him, to have him wrap his arms around me, and comfort me with his words. I am filled with great contentment and wellbeing as I sleep throughout the night safely in his loving arms.

CHPAPTER 19

Texas and Louisiana

I am a little hesitant about writing what I felt is a prophecy concerning Texas, Louisiana, and Bobby Jindal. The Holy Spoke to me and said it is like stepping into a field of land minds. One wrong step and it could blow up on me. You will have to discern for yourself the truth of these words. I was not even sure I heard it right, but I will give it a try.

The Lord is going to save Texas. But one city will fall. But the city that falls will be like the Alamo, and it will give place to the Lord's return. The blood of those that died at the Alamo is once again crying out. There is something about the Alamo that is sacred to the Lord, and he is still honoring their sacrifice. No it is not San Antonio that will fall. I see the enemy getting ready to attack but just as the Israelites were protected by God, I see a fire standing between the Israelites and the enemy. As darkness falls the fire will be lit. Keep your eyes on Texas. If I was a Texan, I would be posting up a sign that says "Remember the Alamo," as a sign crying out to the Lord to once again remember their sacrifice. Texas is going to be given a sign of the Lord's return. Jesus has chosen this state to display this sign.'

Louisiana is another state that will be saved, but once again there is one city in this state that will fall. There is something about Bobby Jindal. All I have received from the Lord is that his name is a sign to the nations about what is to take place. The enemy knows this and is determined to destroy his good name, but do not listen. The people of Louisiana will have to sacrifice in order for their state to be saved, but it will not be in vain. When all looks helpless, the situation will turn around for the Lord will release his angels on her behalf. Sorrow will turn into joy, for the gates of hell will not prevail against her. Because her people will stand up for Jesus, Jesus will stand up for her. Watch Louisiana and Bobby Jindal. Louisiana will become a bright beacon. Somehow I see the web being instrumental in God's plan of salvation for this state. If I was to pick a sign for this state it would be a duck. I would post it in windows, on cars, etc, as a sign that prophetically you will drive the enemy crazy, that the enemy will miss his target. I want to laugh at the enemy because of what the state will do to him. Laugh, Laugh, Laugh in the face of your enemy wants to rise up within me whenever I think of Louisiana, a gut busting belly laugh.

Great will be the fall of those two cities, one is Texas and one in Louisiana. These two states will have great repentance before their Lord. I see a great anvil with heavy chains being laid across it. Then a huge sword swings down, and these chains are then broken in two by divine intervention.

CHAPTER 20

Whispers of His Voice

The Father God, Jesus, the Holy Spirit and I have had many talks. It's a joy to commune with them. The soft whisper of their words can come at any time. Usually for me it is when I am just waking up in the morning, when I am half asleep. There are fewer barriers between us at this time, as the concerns of the day have not yet intruded between us. Just like God is more than God, his words are more than words. Some of the words given to me are as follows:

Flowers and Fragrances

Most women like flowers. We are touched by their rare beauty and extraordinary smell. Jesus also enjoys his flowers. I was given a vision of Jesus slowly walking in his heavenly garden and enjoying the rare beauty and unique fragrances of his flowers. There was joy on his face as he smelled their distinctive fragrances. Jesus revealed to me that each one of us has a flower designed just for us. As he walks among them, he smells their lovely fragrance and we are brought to his remembrance. Jesus' flower is called the Rose of Sharon and Lily of the Valley. In Solomon 2:1 it says, "I AM the rose of Sharon."

At one of my encounters with the Lord, he spoke to me and said that I had a reward waiting for me in heaven, a basket of flowers. It was to be my reward for sharing this truth about his flowers with a friend of mine. Every time we share the spoken word with someone, we will receive a reward. Do not be afraid to share his words with others. "And, behold, I come quickly; and my reward is with me, to give every man according to his work shall be." (Revelation 22:12)

The Lord's garden was created and designed with each flower planted in a particular position radiating its glory. Each person was created with a destiny, purpose and place. Jesus has created a place for us. But place is not just a building, it can be a position to be held. Ask the Lord to explain to you how you can serve him and to show you your place in his kingdom. For evildoers shall be cut off but those that wait upon the Lord, they shall inherit the earth. For yet a little while, and the wicked shall not be; yea thou shalt diligently consider his place, and it shall not be. (Psalm 37:9-10 KJV)

Your Way, His Way

Jesus as master is different from Jesus as Lord. The Apostles called him Lord and master. Give the Lord your way of doing things, and pray that Jesus will give you his way of doing things. Giving control and authority to Jesus as master is to surrender to his rule and control over your life. Accepting his way of doing things is to acknowledge he has the wisdom and knowledge to correctly handle any situation, and that he is much wiser and so much more powerful than you are. Have you ever wondered how Jesus will handle the Battle of Armageddon?

I was given a vision of myself standing at attention. I was dressed in a style of clothing and armor very similar to what was worn by the Roman soldiers during the time of Christ. My linen tunic was cut a little longer than mid thigh, and the color of my tunic was a brilliant white. There was a gold breast plate warn over the tunic, and I had on golden sandals. There was a gold two edged sword raised up high in my hand, and I was ready for battle. All of a sudden the Lord spoke, "Lay your sword down." Before the words were even formed I had my sword laid on the ground. I didn't even think about doing it. It was done instantaneously at the same time the words were spoken. The bible says, "For the word of God is quick, and powerful, and sharper than any two-edged sword." (Hebrews 4:12 KJV) The Lords words are powerful and have great authority. To have authority, you must be under authority. Place yourself under Jesus' authority by surrendering all of your life to him and see what happens.

There are many battles Christian are currently fighting all over the world. But there is coming a time when you will surrender your will to the Father, like Jesus did when he said, "your will not mine be done." (Luke 22:42 KJV) knowing you may not escape death. The word says that judgments are coming soon, and only by absolute surrender to Jesus will you have the authority and power needed to do battle against the enemy. Sometimes the Lord will have you do battle, and sometimes he will battle on your behalf. Allow Jesus to rule and reign in your life, and to determine your ending.

When you give your life to the Lord, your life no longer belongs to you, it belongs to God. A good example of this is a word of knowledge the Holy Spirit gave to me. The Lord spoke to me one day and said because of the mental abuse inflicted upon me, and all the words spoken out of anger against me by my ex-husband, "The curse of war would be upon him for the rest of his life." War means a place where there is death, destruction, fighting, wounds, sometimes victory, and sometimes defeat.

In James 4:1-4 (KJV) it says, "From whence come wars and fighting's among you? come they not hence, even of your lusts that war in your members? Ye lust, and have not: ye kill, and desire to have, and cannot obtain: ye fight and war, yet ye have not, because ye ask not. Ye ask, and receive not, because ye ask amiss, that ye may consume it upon your lusts. Ye adulterers and adulteresses know ye not that the friendship of the world is enmity with God? whosoever therefore will be a friend of the world is the enemy of God."

That pronouncement of judgment bothered me because I had been taught to love our enemies, so I asked the Lord about it. He said, "When his life no longer belongs to him, and he gives his life totally and completely to me, and it is mine; the curse that was placed on his life can no longer be, for his life is no longer his." I believe many people have curses on their life because they have not given their life totally and completely to the Lord. The bible says that, "whosoever is angry with his brother without a cause shall be in danger of the judgment." (Matthew 5:22 KJV)

Walking in the Miraculous

Because of the destruction that I went through, I was always drawn more towards the Father God than Jesus, and I was given a considerable desire to read the Old Testament by the Holy Spirit. I learned to love the Old Testament; as I needed to love my past and not separate myself from it. The Father God became my shelter and safety during that time.

As Jesus poured out his grace and glory, a deep inner healing began manifesting in my life. Sometimes the Lord would reveal an aspect of his life to me, and then following that I was healed in that same area of my own life. Although I was very close to the Father, Jesus was there. One of the words given to me by the Holy Spirit was, "Jesus is the reflection of the Father God, like looking into a clear body of water, and seeing an image reflected back."

After that time of mental abuse in my life, the Lord had to intervene supernaturally to heal me in order to give me a life. The partial amnesia I suffered and all the horrible wounding inflicted upon me would take many years for Jesus to heal. Parts of me had to be resurrected like Lazareth. I was so broken there was nothing left of me. I was confused, afraid, and areas of my life had just vanished, time had vanished. A lot of the ties that bind us to people and events were completely severed. I was thrust into a world of great difficulties, battles, and a lot of healing would be needed; but Jesus was there. Jesus would become my rock to stand upon. How tenderly he held me in his arms during that period of time. I came to know his gentleness and kindness, his great and unfailing love.

I have learned to walk in the miraculous every second of

every day. My Lord corrected misconceptions and taught me many things. I came to know that Jesus created by God and coming forth from a virgin, was a miracle. If Jesus is a miracle and lives inside me and surrounds me, a miracle then exists inside me and surrounds me. If Jesus is the resurrection, then it also follows that the resurrection is inside me and surrounds me. His word says, "I am the resurrection, and the life: he that believeth in me, though he were dead, yet shall he live:" (John 11:25 KJV

Breaking Vows

At times he had to explain the actions of others so I would not take their actions personally. Some teachings are beyond my comprehension to explain, and some I sure you would disagree with.

The Holy Spirit began talking to me one morning about my ex-husband. He shared with me that sometimes an angry husband who strikes out verbally to his wife really is projecting self hatred for himself on you, so do not take it personally. In forgiving him, you are not projecting that same self hatred back towards him so it cannot come back to you, like it will to him.

I also learned an attitude of the heart can become a vow. For many years I had said to myself that I would rather die than ever go back to my ex-husband. One morning I woke up and the Holy Spirit came upon me and out of the blue I said, "I would rather my ex-husband die than me die." At that moment it was a little shocking that I would think such a thing. The Holy Spirit then showed me that when we were first married I was so in love with my ex-husband I was willing to die in order for the Lord to save him. As a result destruction came upon my life.

In order for me to be set free I had to no longer accept death in my life, on his behalf. Jesus showed me that he died and paid the price for my ex-husbands salvation, I did not need to. I had been paying the price all those years. The Lord broke that vow off me, removed the death, and changed the attitude of my heart. I was set free. Now that thought no longer crosses my mind. Sometimes out of love we make foolish vows in our heart that need to be broken.

Freedom

The Lord wants to set us all free, but first we must set the Holy Spirit free to do the work he needs to do. The greatest gift you could ever give the Holy Spirit is to set him free. Many times we bind him to us not allowing him to do the work he would like to do. We want him to do the work we want him to do, what we think is best. Quietly pray to him and pray, "I set you free Holy Spirit to do the work you want to do in my life and in the lives of my loved ones. I'm sorry for stopping you and not allowing you to do the work you needed to do. Please forgive me, in Jesus name, Amen."

In the bible a women was caught in the very act of adultery and brought before the Lord for premature judgment, and for her it would have been immediate death by stoning. According to the law this needed to be carried out. Jesus hearing their demand for the law to be upheld wrote on the ground. The Holy Spirit revealed to me he was signing a contract on the earth promising to die for her sins and others, in order to pardon her and to bring her out from under the curse of the law. It says in Genesis 3:19 (KJV), "that from out of the ground was thou taken," and that man would die and be returned to it for sin. It seems appropriate that he would sign a contract on the earth so mankind would not have to be returned to the dust of the earth for sin, breaking that curse and covenant placed on the earth.

Count the Cost

Many will be afraid or not want to pay the price to follow Jesus when times become difficult. Many will drink bitter water. The bible says to count the cost, "For which of you, intending to build a tower, sitteth not down first, and counteth the cost, whether he have sufficient to finish it?" (Luke 14:28 KJV)

Remember the ten virgins in the bible, where five were foolish and five were wise (Mathew 25:1-13). The wise ones had oil in their lamps and they were ready to enter into his kingdom. The foolish ones had no oil in their lamps so they were not prepared and did not enter into his kingdom when the Lord returned. The Holy Spirit quickened to me that the five wise virgins were willing to pay the cost to enter into the Lord's kingdom, but the foolish virgins were not willing to pay the cost until they had to. As a result, they missed entering into his kingdom.

Another lesson learned in the bible was about Ananias

and Sapphira. They sold a possession and kept back part of the price. Because of their decision, death entered into their life until it was too late to save them. (Acts 5) Do no miss out on everlasting life and spending eternity in heaven with Jesus. Giving all of your life to Jesus and doing it before it is too late is the only answer.

Jesus said in John 12:35-36 to walk with him while the light is with you, or darkness could come upon you and you will not know where you will end up.

Two Walks

One day Jesus appeared to me and said very quietly, "Come walk with me." There are two walks identified in the bible.

One walk is when the Apostles were invited to walk with Jesus. They followed him and lived according to his will. As Jesus was ministering on earth, Jesus invited the rich young ruler to change his life and follow him but the young ruler choose not to.

Then there is the other walk. Instead of us accepting the invitation to walk with Jesus, we walk according to our own will.

After Jesus died the Apostles lived in fear and despair for they no longer knew what their future held. Everything they thought their lives would be was gone. They were living in turmoil, and they did not know what would happen to them, nor did they understand what was transpiring.

In order save Simon and another follower's destiny, Jesus appeared to them on the road to Emmaus and walked with them. He explained the scriptures to them for they did not know that his crucifixion was a part of the Father's will. Jesus came to put them on the right path for their lives.

Do you walk with Jesus and follow him, allowing him to perform his will for your life; or do you walk according to your own will and then cry out to Jesus, to rescue you from difficulties? Would you not rather escape difficulties?

As we walk with Jesus, he manifests his glory in our life. Recently, I was praying about a concern I had, when suddenly I began praying in tongues by the power of the Holy Spirit. Jesus began speaking to me and instantly I was standing beside him. He said, "Let me bring you before the Father so that you can talk to him." I saw myself walking beside Jesus as he brought me before the Father. He was giving me a lesson on what it is like when we pray in the Holy Spirit.

Hebrews 7:25 (KJV) says, "Wherefore he is able also to save them to the uttermost that come unto God by him, seeing he ever liveth to make intercession for them."

Gift for God

The Holy Spirit touched me one day with a heart full of love for the Father. As I was praying, I asked the Holy Spirit if he would show me what would be a precious and special gift that I could give to the Father God who has everything. It was quickened to me that the most precious gift we could give to him would be our spending time with him. To the Father God time with him is more precious than our money. So I prayed for the Holy Spirit to create a special time for me to be with God the Father, to commune with him.

We are so very precious to him and he desires that we spend time with him. Oftentimes, we only spend time in his presence when we need something or have some problem we cannot handle. It would hurt me to have my children only want to talk to me or visit with me if all they did was ask me to give them something.

Just saying, "Hi, I am thinking of you and love you," are precious words. The Lord thinks of us often and desires to commune with us.

30 Pieces of Silver

Like an outlaw in the old west, each one of us has a bounty on our heads. The Holy Spirit quickened to me that because of the bounty or curse on our heads, the enemy hunts us to destroy us, steel from us, bind us, etc. Judus betrayed Jesus for 30 pieces of silver the price that was on his head. Jesus paid that price for each one of us. When you understand and know that Jesus paid the price of 30 pieces of silver for you, and that bounty is no longer on your head, it is then removed and replaced with the 30 fold blessing. Anyone who blesses you will receive 30 fold in return.

Once a person recognizes what Jesus accomplished on the cross and the blessings he has placed upon us, the richness of his glory is then abundantly poured out. The word states that his people are destroyed for lack of knowledge. (Hosea 4:6 KJV) The Lord is opening up his word to his people to better prepare them for the days ahead, to help them survive this "Suddenly" that is coming, and to receive his tremendous blessings that he desires to give them.

All or Part

Many people because of serious hurts and rejections have a fragmented life. One morning Jesus shared an important truth with me. He revealed to me there is a difference between giving your life to God, and giving yourself to God. There is an element missing when you give your life to God, but not yourself. In protecting yourself from hurt, you often miss the most important part of sharing, being one with one another.

Being one with Jesus, knowing him, is the greatest blessing a person can ever have. Just as Jesus is one with the Father, he desires to be one with us. He does not only want to share your life he wants to be a part of you, and have you be a part of him. The word says, "And the glory which thou gavest me I have given them; that they may be one, even as we are one. I in them, and thou in me, that they may be made perfect in one" (John 17:22-23 KJV)

Salvation Assured

I have four daughters whom I absolutely love. About forty years ago when I was going through my time of greatest desperation, Jesus spoke to me from the future and said, "I was already there with him," and then he named two of my children and said they were already there with him. He let me know my third daughter would be saved but she would be saved his way, not my way. I always felt in my heart that she would go through many trials in order to be saved, but what had been predestined for her was meant to be. But

I was comforted with the knowledge that no matter what she went through she would be saved. There is a scripture that says, "And our hope of you is stedfast, knowing, that as ye are partakes of the sufferings, so shall ye be also of the consolation. For God would not have us trust in ourselves." (II Corinthians 1:7,9 KJV)

Then for over 35 years I interceded and prayed for my fourth daughter to be saved. I needed Jesus to assure me she also would be saved. Finally, a few years ago my oldest daughter had a vision where the rapture had happened. Our family was instantly transported to heaven and we were all standing together in a large room. She looked off to the side and saw Jesus quietly sitting in the room. She saw her grandparents, parents, sisters, aunts, cousins, etc., all gathered collectively in his presence.

She became aware as she looked around that two cherished members of her family were missing. This greatly upset her and she slowly approached Jesus with fear filling her heart to talk with him. Jesus looked with compassion upon her and asked her what was wrong. She than brought their names before him and pleaded with him to save them, expressing her grief at their not being there. Jesus with concern and compassion filling his being then answered her supplications and up popped the two family members that were missing; but for her one sister there was going to be much regret when it came to her children. For when my fourth daughter popped up the first words out of her mouth were, "What have I done?" For knowledge and a repent heart will be given to her concerning her children.

Will these two family members be left behind when the

rapture happens, and then go through the tribulation in order to be saved? Or only by tribulation will she and her family enter into the kingdom of heaven? How soon will it start?

The Lord once spoke to me and said I could ask him anything and he would answer me, but sometimes the truth of the answer can hurt so he said be careful what I wanted to ask him. He may not answer immediately, but he will answer your questions.

When this "Suddenly" event happens, Jesus will pour out the absolute assurance of salvation his people will need, letting them know without a doubt that they and their loved ones are already there with him; or he will let his children know which of their family members have not yet entered into his kingdom, in order that prayers and intercession can be made for them. Jesus loves his people and wants them to be extremely happy in heaven. He knows that the desire of their heart is to have their loved ones with them. "The effectual fervent prayer of a righteous man availeth much." (James 5:16 KJV) Nothing is impossible with Jesus.

Question Answered

Why do you suppose we are called the body of Christ? Because of my experience with God at the age of 16, I have come to believe that each person who belongs to Jesus makes up one individual cell of our Lord's body. There are billions of cells in a person's body.

The word says that even the rocks would cry out praise to the Lord if we didn't. I believe each cell in our body cries out praises, rejoices, and worships our Lord. I use to wonder what would keep us from rejecting God once we got to heaven, because the angles once rejected him, so I asked Jesus.

The Holy Spirit quickened to me that in our new resurrected body each cell in our body will have a much greater capacity to praise, rejoice and love the Lord than we do now, so that it will be impossible to reject him as the angels did. It is a very comforting thought to know we can ask him anything and he will answer our questions, and that he has wonderful plans for our life.

Hiding

Jesus sees a lot of hiding going on. Like Adam and Eve, people are hiding their sins from the Lord and others. The Lord is going to expose sin. He will let his people know that he sees the hurt they have inflicted upon others. He is going to bring repentance and righteousness to his people. This is going to forever change their walk with the Lord. This outpouring of the Holy Spirit is going to cause a reverence, fear, and respect for God. Hebrews 12:28 (KJV) says, "let us have grace, whereby we may serve God acceptably with reverence and godly fear."

"The fear of the ungodly is going to explode," is the word I have received from the Lord. However, Jesus will be a refuge and place of safety for the body of Christ. The Lord's people will take shelter in the Lord arms; and there will be no more hiding from the truth. People will have to face the truth that their lives are changed forever, and there is no going back.

"The bricks are fallen and I will rebuild" has been quoted by many of our politicians. When the New York twin towers fell man declared that they were going to build them bigger and better as a sign of man's greatness; but it is really a sign of man's rebellion to God. The belief that man alone can overcome any destruction and come back bigger and better is doomed to failure in the days ahead. Arrogance will be a thing of the past.

There will be a huge undertaking of nations and governments to put things back together once this "Suddenly" happens but unless the Lord builds it, it will not stand.

Hidden Manna

The Lord plans on sharing many mysteries and secrets with his people. The people of Israel faced a time of starvation after Moses led them out of Egypt and into the promised-land. To prevent this starvation God provided them with his manna. Christians will also face their time of starvation as they turn to Jesus and follow him. God's Supernatural wisdom and knowledge will be necessary in order for the Lord's people to survive until he comes. He will pour this manna out upon his people to feed them. As with the Israelites, there will be instructions to follow.

In Revelation, Chapter 2, the Church of Pergamos faced great persecution for their faith and stood up for the word; but they did compromise themselves by worshipping idols and engaging in sexual immorality. Pergamos was told that if they overcame and rejected these actions then the hidden manna from God would be theirs.

Hope and a Future

Like many others I came out of a life of sin and rebellion to God. The choices I made led up to my own destruction. If not for Jesus, I would not have had any hope for the future. Once I invited him into my heart and surrendered my life to him, he took over and turned my life around. Many of the lessons and teachings the Lord imparted to me were taught to bring healing and deliverance into my life, and to give me a life with him. In the days ahead many will encounter Jesus, and walk beside him as he explains and teaches the truth about his kingdom. He does not want a spirit of religion to be a part of your life. He wants an open and honest relationship with you.

Many of you will experience the same great pressures I certainly experienced, but Jesus is greater than any fear or disaster here on earth. The Lord will love you, comfort you, and pour out his spirit upon you to let you know he is there and you are not alone. Even when you don't have faith or trust in him he will provide it.

Window Shopping

People today are window shopping, looking for answers everywhere. They are going here and there to find them. One day Jesus will quietly speak a word to you and you will believe him, or give you a vivid dream to show you something and you will instantly know its meaning. He will activate your faith and give you an expectancy you never had before. You will no longer have to believe what someone else speaks to you for he will reveal things to you himself. You will know him intimately, and he will help you to know yourself. His word says no one will need to teach us for we will all be taught of the Lord.

Hebrews 12:2 (KJV) states that "Jesus is the author and finisher of our faith; who for the joy that was set before him endured the cross, despising the shame, and is set down at the right hand of the throne of God." To God belong all the glory, praise, and honor. Jesus will carry you through all that you will endure until the end. Our help comes from the Lord.

Temple Rebuilt

Jesus' spiritual kingdom and our world join together when we accept Jesus as our savior. It is the merging of two lives and kingdoms. Instead of God just dwelling in the Jewish temple as in David's day, we became the temple. He then dwells within each person who accepts him as Savior.

I believe that soon the temple in Israel will be rebuilt not only as a sign to the Jews of prophecy fulfilled, but to point to a better way. It will point to Jesus who dwells within hearts, who does not need to dwell in buildings. We are the temple of the Holy Spirit, and he dwells within all our being when we accept him as Savior and ask him into our hearts.

Once we ask Jesus into our hearts, Christ begins to repair our hearts, cleans us, and fill us with his presence. It is written, "What? know ye not that your body is the temple of the holy Ghost which is in you, which you have of God, and ye are not your own?" (I Corinthians 6:19 KJV)

Because Jesus dwells within us, the spirit of the anti Christ is being restrained. The revival predicted for the later days will take place leading many to Christ. At the same time the spirit of the anti Christ will increase. He will be determined to eliminate the Lord's people off the face of the earth so that he can rule and reign; and persecution like we have never seen before will take place.

Table Manners

Often Jesus teaches us in parables. I was given a vision of Jesus sitting quietly at a large dinner table, along with me and several others. Jesus was sitting at the head of the table and I was sitting on the right side of the table. I remember there was a white linen table cloth covering the table. No one spoke a word. It seemed Jesus was waiting for something. It took me a few seconds as I evaluated what was happening. I then asked Jesus what could I serve him, was there anything I could get him? A smile and twinkle lit up his eyes as he looked at me. Then he spoke and said," If you could choose any food you wanted to eat, what would your choice be?"

I thought for a moment, and remembered a time thirty years ago when I saw a white beat-up old van sitting by the side of the road, parked near a field of tall dry grass. There was an elderly man sitting behind a small folding card-table with a display of Bing cherries for sale. I stopped and bought two large plastic bags of these cherries, and brought them home. When you looked at these cherries they were perfect in appearance and unblemished. The size was not too large, nor too small, and they were perfectly shaped. They had the richest deep purple color. They were firm, plump, very juicy, and full of rich flavor, the very best I had ever tasted; as I soon found out when I arrived home and tasted them.

Those Bing cherries were so perfect I went back the next day to buy more but the famer was no longer there. I scouted all over the area looking for this farmer. I continued to look each cherry harvesting season canvassing the area for the next few years, but I never saw him again. Remembering those cherries, I asked Jesus for a bowl of Bing cherries.

Then a servant of the Lord brought out to me a bowl of Bing cherries. As I looked down at the bowl of cherries before me, it came to me to ask Jesus if it was all right if I shared them with the other people seated at the table. He was pleased with my response and graciously said yes.

When you are in the presence of the Lord, what is your first thought? Are you waiting to be served or are you serving? Are you willing to share your blessings with others? What are your priorities? Who is the most important person in your life? These are areas of a person's spiritual life that needs to be taught and built up. The kingdom of heaven is about our heart and what comes out of it.

"For the kingdom of God is not meat and drink; but righteousness, peace, and joy in the Holy Ghost." (Romans 14:17 KJV) The foundation is our relationship with Jesus and his place in our life. Serving him should be as natural to us as breathing. Jesus said he came to serve.

A long time ago, I use to think about going to heaven and serving Jesus for all eternity. What would it be like? Would

I be like to be a waitress for all eternity? That did not sound appealing to me? I kept trying to bury the thought inside me and kept pushing it aside. One day the Lord spoke to me and said, "Peachey, serving me means you are not placing yourself above me." Sometimes I can get some really mixed up thoughts going through my head that the Lord has to straighten out.

Matthew 21:27-28 KJV) "And whosoever will be chief among you, let him be your servant: Even as the Son of man came not to be ministered unto, but to minister, and to give his life a ransom for many."

Ask Jesus to create a relationship with him that would produce a heart to serve him, and that you would be a blessing to others, and not to always think of yourselves first.

Better Person

The Lord gave me a teaching one day about becoming a better person. He spoke to me and said that when Jesus reveals a part of himself to you and he comes into your life in that area, you become a better man, women, or child in that area.

If a person struggles with homosexuality, as they invite Jesus into different elements of their life and become one with him, they once again become what God created them to be. A person needs to open up their heart and allow Jesus to come in and dwell within them, changing them according to his will.

For a Homosexual, it could be as simple as embracing life; having Jesus coming into that one area of embracing life. Or maybe you were wishing, as a child, you were someone else of the opposite sex, because you thought that other person was more loved; so Jesus needs to come in to that area and show you that you are loved for who you are. Then again, maybe as a child you were rejected totally by one parent, so you seek that relationship of the same sex.

Jesus understands the areas he needs to go into to deliver a person. In order to be delivered, a person may need a great deal of healing. We have so many areas of our life where a person can be wounded, they are too numerous to number. The Lord may hate sin, but he loves the sinner with all his hearts.

The Lord once spoke to me and said, "He does not judge or deal with his children according to our sin, but he deals with us according to his will."

Jesus does not want to became a dictator in your life telling you what to do, he wants to set people free, healing and delivering them. It is not always easy to be set free to put people on the right path for their life.

Many people do not know what they lack in their relationship with Jesus, their family members, or each other. Ask Jesus to come into all areas of your life. As a person grows in Jesus they change and become a better person. To know Jesus is to spend time with him. We learn of him by reading his word. Where your treasure is that is where your focus will be.

Remember when the Israelites were going to the Promised Land. They could only go in and conquer the land a little at a time, or they could not hold it. Becoming a Christian is a lifelong process of knowing Jesus. It is not about rules and regulations because Jesus knew we could not keep the law. It is a matter of the heart.

Jesus said, "I will never leave thee, nor forsake thee. (Hebrews 13:5 KJV)

CHAPTER 21

The Final Word

As I was thinking about the ending of this book, the Lord witnessed to me that he would like to write the "final words" of this book; so I wrote the words down as he spoke them to me.

He would say, "Learn to care for one another. I am going to place my seal upon the foreheads of my people. They will be sealed against the 'day of judgment' that is coming soon upon the earth. Tempt not the Lord thy God in all that you ask of him. The enemy is not your friend, and he is actively seeking out those to follow him. Just before the destruction of my body, I asked my Apostles to pray, but they would not stay awake. Once again I asked my people to pray, to stay awake as this sudden destruction is almost here. Yet, are not my people also falling asleep. The spirit is willing, but the flesh is weak.

As I did not abandon my Peter then, I will not abandon my people now. Just as I poured out my Holy Spirit in the upper room as a sign of my coming, I will also pour out my spirit in these last days. My spirit will testify of me, he will glorify me. Watch and wait for the outpouring of my spirit.

You are called my faithful ones, my chosen ones. Holy unto the Lord are you. Nothing will stop the outpouring of my Holy Spirit during the last days. The enemy will try but he has already failed. I will not fail you. I will not fail you.

You have passed from death to life. One day you will stand in my presence and I will say to you, 'good and faithful servant, enter into my kingdom which I have prepared for you before the foundation of the world. Trust in me, believe in me for I will not abandon you, nor will I forsake you. My strength I will give unto you, my peace that passes all understanding is yours. I will light your way in the dark days ahead, I will be there to comfort you, to love you, to care for you.

In the beginning Peter denied me, but came back to me in repentance. I did not deny him. My mercy is over all. Thus sayeth the Lord."

COMING SOON

Book coming:

His Breath
Faith for Earth's Final Hours

I see the title for my third and probably final book in this series as, "His Breath." It is about faith for earth's final hours. The Lord has only given me a distant glimpse of what this book will be about.

God's breath is about the most important part of mankind, without it we could not live. As Jesus died on the cross and released his last breath, it was finished. His breath then departed into all the earth to bring life, not to bring death. Man has not recognized the breath of God. Man cannot see his breath but it is there. His breath brings joy and light into the world.

Satan tried to stop the breath of God by crucifying Christ. But the breath is eternal and cannot be killed, nor can you separate it from God. The Father, Son, and Holy Spirit are one, each unique in their own way. If you kill the soul does the breath die? Or if you kill the spirit of man does it die? These questions and answers will be coming in this third book.

The Father God gave to me this message for his people. Thus says the Lord, "The Holy Spirit is being released to answer many questions in the last days. Jesus died to answer many questions he knew were coming. The Spirit of Truth and the Spirit of Death will both operate during the days to come. Inherit my kingdom, or inherit the Devil's kingdom, those are the two choices that will be presented during these final hours.

Jesus, my Son, during his final hours had a choice to make, to accept my will for his life or not to accept my will. Many will be faced with the same decision my son made. Which will you choose?

My heart breaks for my people knowing what they will soon go through on behalf of my Son. Just as my heart broke when my son died on the cross so will your heart break with the message of the cross that will be given to your loved ones, and what they will face. But my glory will surround my chosen ones, and my crown will be placed upon their head. Do not be afraid. My Son removed the fear by the things which he suffered and had to endure. He knew the enemy would be defeated, and so shall you know as you face your finest hours. Thus sayeth the Lord God Almighty, Creator of heaven and earth."

Book coming: (mayby)

As I was praying about the next book to write, Jesus gave me the words, "Dreams." Over the last 40 years Jesus has gifted me with many dreams and visions about Himself, angels, rulers, future events, etc. This book would be an unveiling of the prophetic on how the Holy Spirit can and will speak to his people today. May the Lord impart to me his spirit of grace to co-labor with him on this second book.

I pray that my Father would bless everyone abundantly who reads "In the Twinkling of His eye."

Peachey

Printed in the United States
By Bookmasters